SECULAR WORK
IS FULL·TIME
SERVICE

SECULAR WORK IS FULL·TIME SERVICE

By Larry Peabody

CHRISTIAN LITERATURE CRUSADE
Fort Washington, Pennsylvania 19034

CHRISTIAN LITERATURE CRUSADE

U.S.A.
P.O. Box 1449, Fort Washington, PA 19034

BRITAIN
51 The Dean, Alresford, Hants., SO24 9BJ

AUSTRALIA
P.O. Box 91, Pennant Hills, N.S.W. 2120

NEW ZEALAND
P.O. Box 1203, Palmerston North

ISBN 0-87508-448-6

Copyright © 1974
Christian Literature Crusade
Fort Washington, PA
This Printing 1994

Quotations from:
The King James Version of the Bible in the Foreword.
The New American Standard Bible (except as otherwise indicated)
   by permission of The Lockman Foundation.
The Modern Language Bible (Berkeley Version). Copyright © 1945,
   1959, 1969, by Zondervan Publishing House. Used by permission.
The New Testament in the Language of the People by Charles B.
   Williams. Copyright © 1966 by Edith S. Williams. Published by
   Moody Press. Moody Bible Institute of Chicago. Used by permission.

PRINTED IN THE UNITED STATES OF AMERICA

To Paul Ludwig
whose life speaks the message
of this book.

CONTENTS

FOREWORD 7

INTRODUCTION 9

1. NO ONE CAN SERVE TWO MASTERS 11

2. ASSIGNMENT: BABYLON 21

3. UP ON THE LAMPSTAND 29

4. THE DAILY GRIND 36

5. TRIMMING THE LAMPS 46

6. GLOWING WITHOUT GLARING 57

7. LIGHT HOUSEKEEPING 68

8. SECRETS OF A LIGHT HEAVYWEIGHT 78

9. THE ADDED THINGS 93

10. THE REST AREAS 104

11. THE CHURCH IN THE WORKPLACE 118

12. HELP WANTED: SPIRITUAL GROWNUPS ... 128

FOREWORD

ONE OF THE INEVITABLE BY-PRODUCTS of materialism is boredom. The materialist must work to acquire more and more, but his work gives him no joy, and that which he acquires through it no satisfaction. He is ever searching for fulfillment, but never finding it. "Why do you spend money for that which is not bread, and your labour for that which does not satisfy?" cried the prophet.

The tragedy is that the materialistic spirit has seeped into the church. Christianity is looked upon by many of its professed adherents as a spiritual addendum to the secular life. So the Christian lives his life during the week like anybody else, but on Sunday he goes to church instead of golf. What a travesty of New Testament Christianity!

"Speak to the people all the words of this life." So spoke the Lord's angel to the first apostles after releasing them from the prison. Christianity is not a religious appendage. It is not merely a fine philosophy. It is *a life*—something that has to be lived 24 hours a day, and 365 days a year.

This book puts a finger on some of the major weaknesses of modern Christianity. One of these is the tendency to departmentalize our lives and confine the spiritual to its own little watertight compartment instead of letting it out to invade and transform the secular. I am reminded of the truth that Brother Lawrence discovered centuries ago, that he could enjoy *The Practice of the Presence of God* as much when he did his chores in the monastery kitchen as when he meditated in the cloisters.

This book has an important message for the believer who feels that he is sentenced to being a second-class citizen in the kingdom of God simply because he finds his daily calling in the secular world. If he is bored and frustrated with the work that God has given him to do, he will find here the path to joyful fulfillment. It is transforming to discover that the secular is sacred when God puts it into your hand, and that in working for that demanding earthly employer one is serving the Lord Christ. This book proves that there is no scriptural authority for the belief that serving God in business is any less spiritual than serving God in full-time ministry.

For this reason it should provide a needed corrective to a trend among some young Christians caught up in the current move of the Spirit to abandon their secular careers and callings under the mistaken impression that "full-time service" is the only worthwhile job for the dedicated Christian.

Larry Peabody has given us something which is biblical and balanced, thought-provoking and challenging. I believe that what my friend is saying in this book is a very important aspect of what the Spirit is saying to the churches today. "He who has an ear, let him hear."

ARTHUR WALLIS

INTRODUCTION

ON SEVERAL OCCASIONS as this book was being written friends asked what it was about. I often answered that the book's purpose is to show how a Christian's faith relates to his everyday work. Sometimes I mentioned the great gulf that separates the Sunday morning church service from the activities in the work place Monday through Friday, adding, "It seems that church is church and work is work . . ."

". . . and never the twain shall meet," came the response with a knowing nod.

What is it that keeps the "twain" apart? I am convinced that our false division of labor into "sacred" and "secular" categories is one of the major reasons that the "twain" so seldom meet. In countless ways the Christian in "secular" work is led to believe his occupation is spiritually second-rate to "full-time Christian service." Such thinking results in great loss to the Kingdom of God. Seeing "secular" work as second-best, seeing the ordinary job as a built-in limitation to serving God full time, will cripple the Christian in his faith and in his work. Many "limping" Christians have stumbled over the man-made dividing line.

A syndicated newspaper columnist recently remarked in print that the modern business office has become the "social center" of life. If this is true, if the life of the world today largely revolves around its work places, then the people of God should permeate those places with salt and light. Such permeation is no second-rate calling. It demands high-caliber Christians. It must have top priority. And it will require a new vision of ordinary work.

Throughout this book the reference point has been the Scriptures, not personal anecdotes and experiences. The Church is "built upon the foundation of the apostles and prophets" (Ephesians 2: 20), and therefore their words should always serve as base line and starting point for whatever we do or teach. Jesus, in praying for His apostles, indicated that it would be "through their word" that the household of faith would grow (John 17: 20). We have their words in Scripture. This book attempts to correct a subnormal view of ordinary work—another reason for reliance upon the Scriptures, since correction is one of its major uses (2 Timothy 3: 16).

In writing these chapters I have been acutely aware of the dangers inherent in any attempt to correct an imbalance. By focusing upon work, the rest of life is thrown temporarily out of focus. Work is by no means the sum total of life, though it comprises a major share of it. This book spotlights "secular" work. However, it is written in full recognition of the importance of those ministries we normally refer to as "full-time Christian service." My goal has not been to set the one type of service over against the other. Rather, it has been to help each of us to see with clearer vision God's purposes in putting so many of His saints to work in the world.

The book is offered to those in ordinary work with the prayer that the Holy Spirit may use it to transform their daily tasks into worship and service to God. It is offered to those who teach in the hope that they may communicate to others God's New Testament plan for men to live unified lives, whole lives, instead of lives fragmented into "sacred" and "secular" halves.

OLYMPIA, WASH.   LARRY PEABODY

1

NO ONE CAN SERVE TWO MASTERS

A BUSINESSMAN ONCE CONFIDED to the president of a seminary: "Sometimes I think I'd like to sell my agency and become the business manager of a Christian organization where I could *really* serve the Lord in my work."

This man's statement reveals an underlying assumption: that a person can't really serve God in his work unless he engages in *full-time Christian service*. Many of us share this assumption about our own everyday work. Secretly we may begrudge having to serve an earthly employer, believing that such work cuts into time that might otherwise be spent serving God. Had we been serious about serving God in a total way, we think, we'd have chosen a career as a minister, a missionary, or a staff person for a Christian organization.

In spite of our inner reservations, most of us continue working in everyday employment. Yet the question still troubles us: Wouldn't it be better to get into something that would allow us to devote more hours to Christian work?

This is an important question, one that needs a scriptural answer. The Christian who works at a job which demands forty hours or more each week devotes over a third of his waking hours to his occupation. Much of his and his family's life style is dictated by his job. Month by month his work schedule makes its regular withdrawal from his limited fund of time. The hours a man spends at work are not the leftovers, either. They are the *prime-time* hours taken from the heart of the day when his energy level and capacity for productive labor are at their peak. If a person is to accomplish anything worthwhile in this life, it will probably be done as he devotes large blocks of this prime time to the task. Can we then, in good conscience, give so many valuable hours to *secular* work?

Then, too, the number of Christians working in ordinary jobs far exceeds the number who labor in what are known as religious occupations. Simple arithmetic makes it clear that most of the prime-time hours of the members of the Body of Christ are given over to worldly concerns, to businesses focused more on time than eternity. Are these hours wasted? Would it be better if most of God's people could get out of ordinary work and into more spiritual employment?

On the surface the answer might appear to be: "Yes —how much more could be accomplished if most of us were in full-time Christian service." Comparing the daily agenda of a pastor with that of a businessman seems to leave little question as to which goes further in serving God. At the end of the day the pastor goes to bed thankful for having spent another whole day in God's service. But the businessman may lie awake and review a day that seems largely a loss spiritually, except for the hour he spent in a church meeting. As he ponders, he may feel he is trying to serve two masters: working for his earthly employer from 8 a.m. to 5 p.m. weekdays, and for God evenings and weekends.

"No one can serve two masters," Jesus said, "for either he will hate the one and love the other, or he will hold to one and despise the other" (Matthew 6:24). Jesus applied this truth to riches. It applies also to our everyday work. If we see our lives as divided into sacred and secular parts, we will try to serve man (our earthly employers) in the one part, and God in the other. But as Jesus has made clear, divided service like this produces inner conflict. The person who loves organized Christian activity will soon see everyday work as an interruption to his "real" mission, and the person who is devoted to his ordinary job will come to regard religious work as a burdensome duty. No one can serve two masters.

Trying to serve two masters leads easily to double-mindedness. A Christian who doubts that his daily chores have much lasting consequence may overextend himself in church activities and programs in his off-hours. After all, *something* has to count for God! He may dream of entering some kind of Christian employment where he can "really serve God in his work," losing all zest for the job at hand. There are seldom sufficient hours in the day for such a man. He lives under the anxiety of never being able to do enough for God because so much of his best time seems spiritually nonproductive. His view of his work leaves him torn between the worthwhile and the meaningless, between the spiritual and the secular poles.

Double-minded Christians are vulnerable, easily thrown by the waves of uncertainty surrounding their work. Unanswered questions breed doubts which undermine faith's operation in the work place. Aren't those who've been "called" more valuable in God's service than those who haven't? Doesn't the typical job bring a person into dangerously close contact with the world and all the evils it represents? Isn't it really more spiritual to "live by faith" than to work for wages? Scripture tells us that a double-minded man is "unstable in all his ways" (James 1: 8).

How, then, may we leave our double-mindedness and arrive at singleness of mind concerning our lifework?

Where can we find stability? Our problem is a matter of vision. Too many of us see our work as it has been pictured by man-made religious teachings. Our vision of work has been earthly, human, man-centered. Single-mindedness and stability come only through God-given vision.

It will help us, if we would see our work as God sees it, to understand one of the revolutionary changes that occurred between the Old Testament and the New. In the Old Testament we see the first steps taken by the Holy God to reclaim the world from the slavery imposed by Satan. After sin entered the world, nothing in it was holy. Everything had become unclean. The entire earth suffered from God's curse.

Then, out of all earth's unclean inhabitants, God set apart the Israelites. After removing them from the uncleanness surrounding them in Egypt, God began showing these people something of the meaning of holiness, cleanness. He had to start with very basic lessons. The "elementary schoolteacher" was God's Law, given through Moses. Under Law, one of the basic lessons was the difference between the sacred and the secular, the clean and the unclean. The Israelites were not yet ready to grasp a full vision of His holiness, so God declared only certain things as clean, dedicated for His use. The priests of the Old Testament were to "distinguish between holy and secular, between clean and unclean" (Leviticus 10: 10, *The Berkeley Version*). The priests were also to "teach My people the difference between the sacred and the secular and show them how to distinguish between the unclean and the clean" (Ezekiel 44: 23, *The Berkeley Version*).

What do the terms secular (or profane) and unclean imply? Anything sacred or clean was that which was accepted by God and set apart (made holy, sanctified) for His purposes. Anything not sacred was therefore secular, common, profane, or unclean. The *Oxford English Dictionary* defines secular as: "Belonging to the world and its affairs as distinguished from the church and religion; civil, lay, temporal. Chiefly used as a negative term, with the meaning non-ecclesiastical, non-religious, or non-sacred."

What were some of the sacred/secular distinctions which the Old Testament priests were to make and to teach? Perhaps the best known is the Sabbath, the day set apart as the Lord's holy day (Exodus 20: 8). The other six days were for common, worldly purposes: therefore they were secular days. A distinction was made between foods—some were clean, some were unclean (Leviticus 11). Places were also divided between the sacred and secular. The Tabernacle had its "holy place" (Leviticus 16: 17), as did the Temple (2 Chronicles 29: 5, 7).

Even in the matter of vocation Old Testament Law distinguished between the holy and the common. In Numbers 16 Korah took Moses and Aaron to task for setting themselves above the common Jews. Korah claimed that "all the congregation are holy, every one of them." To which Moses answered, "the Lord will show . . . who is holy, and will bring him near to Himself." The next day the Lord told Moses and Aaron: "Separate yourselves from among this congregation, that I may consume them instantly" (v. 21). Moses and Aaron pleaded with God to spare the congregation. As a result, only Korah and his fellow rebels were exterminated—for the sin of grumbling against the Lord's distinction in the matter of vocations.

But these sacred/secular distinctions of the Jewish Law were only temporary. God's people in the Old Testament were "held in bondage under the elemental things of the world. But when the fulness of time came, God sent forth His Son . . . in order that He might redeem those who were under the Law . . ." (Galatians 4: 3–5). Praise God! the fullness of time has come. God's Son has triumphed over all uncleanness. As a result, when the Spirit of Christ inhabits a person, that person's whole life is now to be seen as clean and sacred. Old Testament distinctions fade away as the light of the New Testament shines upon them.

Days? Jesus is Lord of the Sabbath. "Therefore let no one act as your judge in regard to food or drink or in respect to a festival or a new moon or a Sabbath day —things which are a mere shadow of what is to come . . ." (Colossians 2: 16, 17). Paul indicated that observing days was a sign of enslavement to "weak and worthless elemental things" (Galatians 4: 9, 10).

Food? Jesus "declared all foods clean" (Mark 7: 19). And Peter was told plainly: "What God has cleansed, no longer consider unholy" (Acts 10: 15).

Places? When the Samaritan woman brought up the issue of holy places, Jesus answered: "Woman, believe Me, an hour is coming when neither in this mountain, nor in Jerusalem, shall you worship the Father. . . . But an hour is coming, and now is, when the true worshipers shall worship the Father in spirit and truth . . ." (John 4: 21, 23). The bodies of Christians have become God's temples in this age (1 Corinthians 6: 19).

Vocations? The New Testament teaches that Christians are "a holy priesthood" (1 Peter 2: 5), and that Jesus Christ "has made us to be . . . priests" (Revelation 1: 6). There are no longer two classes of God's people. Today none of God's people are to be "considered unclean and . . . excluded from the priesthood" as so many were in the Old Testament (Ezra 2: 62). All believers are holy. All are priests.

A small action taken by Jesus demonstrates the profound difference between the Old and New Testaments in the matter of the clean and unclean, the sacred versus the secular. Lepers, under Jewish Law, were unclean, required to be separated from the people, shunned at all costs. The priests who examined them only looked at their sores. Even Elisha, in healing Naaman from leprosy, sent him away to wash (2 Kings 5: 10). But Jesus did not stop with a mere look at the leper who came to Him. Jesus did not send him away or shun his company. Jesus *touched* him! An unthinkable act for an Old Testament Jew! Jesus was not contaminated by touching the leper. Instead, the leper was made clean. What power there is in that life! Whatever Jesus touches is made clean. When our lives are touched by Jesus, the unclean is made clean. God intends that all we are, all we own, and all we do be set apart, made holy, for His purposes. In the life of a Christian, then, no place remains for *sacred* or *secular* labels.

In the New Testament God does not depict the Christian life as divided into *sacred* and *secular* parts. Rather, He shows it as a unified life, one of wholeness, in which we may single-mindedly serve Him, even in our everyday work. The glorious, liberating truth is that in Christ God has performed the impossible. In Christ, that which was once secular has become sacred. The wall between them has been removed. "For *everything* created by God is good, and nothing is to be rejected, if it is received with gratitude: for it is sanctified by means of the word of God and prayer" (1 Timothy 4: 4, 5).

Jesus said, "*All things* have been handed over to Me by My Father" (Matthew 11: 27). According to Hebrews 2: 8 and 9, God has put *all things* in subjection to Jesus Christ. And only because this is true can the Christian "do *all* in the name of the Lord Jesus" (Colossians 3: 17). The New Testament fairly rings with the words, "all things." Paul wrote that "*all things* belong to you, whether . . . things present or things to come; *all things* belong to you, and you belong to Christ; and Christ belongs to God" (1 Corinthians 3: 21–23). "God causes *all things* to work together for good to those who love God, to those who are called according to His purpose" (Romans 8: 28). Jesus has "ascended far above all the heavens, that He might fill *all things*" (Ephesians 4: 10). And as a result, we Christians are enabled to live so that "in *all things* God may be glorified through Jesus Christ" (1 Peter 4: 11).

Your everyday work and mine must be included among the "all things" that we now claim for God's kingdom through Christ. And since our ordinary work belongs to God, we make the delightful discovery that we serve only one Master—our heavenly Employer. We might even say, "God owns the company that employs me." It is because these earthly enterprises belong to God that we employees can "be obedient to those who are [our] masters according to the flesh . . . *as to Christ*" (Ephesians 6: 5). For the moment God may have delegated some of His authority to the earthly supervisor for whom we work. But since all things belong to God, that supervisor is simply God's agent, even if an unbeliever. (This is not to say that nonbelievers will inherit salvation, only that God will accomplish His purposes even through those who reject Christ.) Each of us, whether one of the bosses or one of the bossed, must ultimately report to the One who owns all things.

The New Testament draws no sacred/secular lines between Christians in *full-time service* and those in other types of work. In fact, the Bible does not contain the phrase "full-time Christian service." It teaches that all Christians should serve God full time, even though our differing vocations display such service in a variety of forms.

It is true that some Christians are "set apart" for the gospel (Romans 1: 1; Acts 13: 2). But this setting apart does not always mean total abstinence from ordinary work. Paul was set apart for gospel service, yet he frequently supported himself by working at a trade. Neither does this setting apart imply any distinction between sacred and secular. All God's people share in Christ's holiness. All Christians are thus set apart for God's use. And from among these holy ones (saints) God selects some for the work of the gospel. The Greek word used for "set apart" in Romans 1: 1 and Acts 13:2 is not the word used for holiness. There is a difference in function between gospel work and ordinary work, but no difference in acceptability before God.

Gospel workers might be compared to government extension agents. These agents are employed to extend reliable information (especially agricultural information) throughout the nation. Their work is to promote the use of improved farming methods. Other men devote their time to farming. Both the farmer and the extension agent contribute to the goal of the government—increasing the level of agricultural productivity.

In a similar way God selects some Christians for gospel extension work and some for work in the ordinary vocations of life. Every Christian should regard his work as sacred. Every Christian should work for God full time. In one way or another, each of us should contribute to God's grand purpose—the building up of the Body of Christ, the Church.

In Scripture God has revealed to us the meaning of work. All work has meaning, whether it be scrubbing a floor or managing a corporation. It is vitally important that we understand the meaning of work as God understands it. In our day of rapid social change, many long-accepted values are being challenged. The work ethic is under attack in the world. Many people despise their jobs, seeing no meaning in mundane tasks. But how can the world ever nave an inkling of the true meaning of work unless it gets it from the Church? It is unthinkable that God's people should view ordinary work as second-best, as less significant than gospel work. As Christians we are to reveal to the world God's plan for the lives of men. Most men spend the bulk of their lives in the ordinary vocations. A large part of our task as Christians, then, will be to help men to see the meaning of their work in the light of what Christ has accomplished. It will not be enough to tell them; we must also show them by our lives.

In Daniel, Scripture pictures a man in ordinary work whose life brought much glory to God. Living as so many of us must in the midst of an ungodly environment, Daniel was described even by pagans as a man "in whom is a spirit of the holy gods" (Daniel 5: 11). Though Daniel worked under earthly supervision, he served only one Master. He did not serve men during prime time and God in his off-hours. This was recognized by one of his earthly employers, King Darius, who acknowledged to Daniel that it was "God, whom you constantly serve" (Daniel 6: 20). There is much that we who work in the world may learn from the life of this man, Daniel, who single-mindedly served his God while an employee of the government in a place called Babylon.

2

ASSIGNMENT: BABYLON

DOES GOD ACTUALLY ASSIGN HIS PEOPLE to ordinary employments as His first choice for their lives? Two common, yet mistaken, ideas make this concept difficult for many Christians to accept. One idea is that a person needs a fairly dramatic "call" if his work is to be used of God. The second idea is that the world, because it is so full of uncleanness, ought to be avoided whenever possible.

Most of us who have been Christians for any length of time are familiar with the term "call." Paul was called to be an apostle (Romans 1: 1; 1 Corinthians 1: 1). We've heard missionaries tell of their own personal Damascus experiences through which they knew God wanted them in foreign missions. Pastors frequently recount the circumstances surrounding their call to this ministry.

On the other hand we rarely, if ever, hear the typical Christian tell of being called by God into his present occupation. Thus we easily assume that those in gospel work have been called, while those in ordinary employment have not. But such a separation of God's people into groups of "those with" and "those without" perpetuates our double vision. It further divides life into sacred and secular segments. It suggests that the called one is of great usefulness to God, while anyone else is useful only in a part-time, odds-and-ends way. To some, the lack of a call into gospel work may even seem to be evidence that the "uncalled" man or woman just wasn't listening. But this idea needs to be tested and examined in the light of Scripture.

Daniel was a man "highly esteemed" by God (Daniel 9: 23; 10: 11, 19), and one through whom God revealed much of His future plan for His people. Yet the Bible does not record any dramatic call of God coming to Daniel which could be compared with the summoning of Paul the apostle. No blinding light struck Daniel to the ground. No voice thundered from heaven telling him to proceed to Babylon. Daniel and his friends did not migrate to Babylon because they saw a spiritual need in that foreign land. No—Daniel, Hananiah, Mishael, and Azariah were the "victims" of circumstances.

Nebuchadnezzar, king of the great Babylonian empire, laid seige to Jerusalem in the third year of Jehoiakim's reign as king of Judah. The city fell and Nebuchadnezzar carried off many of its citizens, including some good-looking, intelligent young Jews to serve in his royal court. And so, in company with the other exiles, Daniel and his friends were deported to Babylon.

From all natural appearances, this transfer from Jerusalem to Babylon was the furthest thing from a call of God. It certainly bore little outward resemblance to Jeremiah's experience when the Lord told him: "Before I formed you in the womb I knew you, and before you were born I consecrated you; I have appointed you a prophet to the nations" (Jeremiah 1: 5). How easily a Jewish exile might have concluded: "If only I'd been called like Jeremiah. Here God has allowed him to stay in Jerusalem, while I go off to Babylon, one of the most corrupt spots on earth. There certainly doesn't seem to be much I can do for God in *this* place."

But if any Jewish exile felt uncalled of God, he was

seeing with eyes of flesh, not eyes of faith. Who was it that carried off the exiles into Babylon? Was Nebuchadnezzar really behind it all? "Thus says the Lord of Hosts, the God of Israel, to all the exiles whom *I* have sent into exile from Jerusalem to Babylon . . ." (Jeremiah 29: 4). Nebuchad-nezzar was only a tool, a convenient instrument. God Himself called these Jews to Babylon. Daniel, the man "highly esteemed" by God, went right along with the worst of the Jews.

The dramatic callings of Paul and Jeremiah were sacred and precious experiences—not because they were dra-matic, but because they came from God Himself. The same God carried off the exiles into Babylon. Was theirs, then, any less a calling? Since their place in life was also outlined by God, was it any less sacred or precious?

Our God of infinite variety uses many means of posi-tioning His people. Some of the methods He uses appear to us to be dramatic, others commonplace. Some methods He uses every day, others only rarely. The calling of the typical Christian who works in a field, factory, or office may, like that of Daniel, come more through an outwork-ing of circumstances than through a spectacular experi-ence. To the eye of the flesh it may appear that one's occupation is explainable in terms of natural causes and effects. Yet the Scriptures assure us that it is God who causes all circumstances to work together for good in the lives of those who love Him. We who love God are positioned not according to human design, nor simply as a result of our own efforts to arrange circumstances, but as a result of God's working. God calls us according to *His* purpose, not ours. We may never be able to understand why God has put some particular Christian in a certain position or occupation. But God's thoughts are not our thoughts, nor are His ways our ways.

According to human thinking it doesn't seem logical to

call a Christian to holy living and then place him in an ungodly environment. "Politics is no place for a Christian," people sometimes say. "It's just too dirty a game."

A statement like this reflects a view of the world which is not uncommon among God's people. In this view, since the world is so unclean, it ought to be avoided as much as possible. Certain legitimate occupations are thought to be so hopelessly corrupt as to be shunned at all costs. For that matter, just about any ordinary job in the world would appear to be tainted. God's name, if used at all, is often taken in vain. Co-workers drink too much at office parties. They tell obscene stories and circulate raw cartoons. Cheating and lying are commonplace. Many women dress in styles designed to tantalize the flesh. Gossip runs rampant, and deep-seated hostilities are cloaked with phony smiles. Selfish ambition and the love of money spur men to scratch and scramble over one another to reach the top. All this and more can be found in the typical work place. Galatians 5: 19–21, with its portrait of the flesh at work, accurately pictures conditions in a modern shop or office.

On the other hand, people in Christian organizations, churches, and mission boards are expected to live above all this. Working elbow-to-elbow with Christians appears so clean in comparison with working in the worldly environment. Leaving ordinary work and joining a Christian organization might seem like quitting the coal mines for a job in an operating room. Therefore, according to this view, entering some form of gospel work is preferable. Doesn't the Bible say that pure and undefiled religion means "to keep oneself unstained by the world" (James 1: 27)? But it was just this view of the world that once led the spiritually inclined into monasteries.

Escape from the world is not God's plan for the Christian. We are not to flee from the world—we are to overcome it. The world is not a thing to be avoided, it is our assignment. Scripture is clear on this point. When Jesus prayed for His followers, He said: "I do not ask Thee to take them out of the world, but to keep them from the evil one" (John 17: 15). Paul, in an earlier letter to the Church of Corinth, instructed them not to associate with so-called Christians who lived immoral lives. Later he had to clarify what he meant, because some had apparently thought they were to shun immoral non-Christians. He explained: "I wrote you in my letter not to associate with immoral people; I did not at all mean with the immoral people of this world, or with the covetous and swindlers, or with idolaters; for then you would have to go out of the world" (1 Corinthians 5: 9, 10). Obviously, getting away from the world was not Paul's idea of overcoming it.

Our pattern has been set. When God the Father prepared a body for Jesus, His Son, He sent that body into the world. Today the Church is Jesus' Body on earth. This Body, like His other body, is sent into the world. Not to some secure and sheltered holy place, but into the degraded world. Our 20th-century world has grown complex. It contains many "worlds." We speak of the "world of banking and finance," or of the "automotive world," or of the "worlds" of government and big business. The call into today's world must include all the components of this complicated planet. Some of these may seem just too polluted for Christian habitation, but we are not to be defeatists. "Do not be overcome by evil, but overcome evil with good" (Romans 12: 21). Jesus overcame the world (John 16: 33). And He expects us to do the same. "For whatever is born of God overcomes the world; and this is the victory that has overcome the world—our faith. And who is the one who overcomes the world, but he who believes that Jesus is the Son of God?" (1 John 5: 4, 5).

Daniel overcame the world even though he was assigned to Babylon. There was little, if anything, in Babylon that appealed to Daniel. He saw the royal menu as something that would contaminate him (Daniel 1: 8). Around him were great numbers of practicing magicians, astrologers, and sorcerers (2: 2), whose actions were strictly forbidden by God's Law (Deuteronomy 18: 10–12). His co-workers were treacherous (6: 4–9), given to drunken parties and idolatry (5: 1–4). Daniel's supervisors ranged from cringingly fearful (1: 10), to exceedingly vain (4: 30), to incredibly gullible (6: 6–9). Babylon was no paradise for this devoted Jew who longed to serve God with his whole heart.

Yet it was to Babylon, vainly pursuing fleshly greatness instead of holiness, that Daniel was called. His occupation even carried him into politics. But Daniel was not stained by the moral filth surrounding him. He overcame the world, not after removing himself to some pure environment but while working right in the thick of the corruption. (While Daniel's work brought him into contact with corruption, the job itself was legitimate. There are, of course, certain occupations which are out-of-bounds for the Christian. Our work and its aims must not contradict basic God-given principles.)

For Daniel, separation from the world took place in the heart. Separation to him did not mean physical isolation from worldly influences. Many years before Daniel's time the prophet Isaiah had written: "Go forth from Babylon! Flee from the Chaldeans!" (Isaiah 48: 20). Daniel made no attempt to remove himself physically from Babylon, yet in spirit he obeyed this word from the Lord. Scripture tells us that Daniel "made up his mind that he would not defile himself with the king's choice food or with the wine which he drank; so he sought permission from the commander of the officials that he might not defile himself (Daniel 1: 8). This determination was reached in Daniel's heart. Through faith in God he overcame evil with good—even while fully involved with the world in his occupation.

The Babylon of today's world is fully as corrupt as it was in Daniel's day. Modern men still chase after greatness and the outward display of power without a care for holiness. There are still abundant opportunities in the world of work to feed the desires of the flesh. But for the man who sees his flesh as having been crucified with Christ, such opportunities appear as hindrances, not attractions.

What, then, would prompt a spiritual man to take a job within this corrupt world system? An order from his King. This, in itself, is sufficient motivation. And it is here, in the heart's motivation, that genuine separation from the world begins. Ask the men of the world why they work. One will say, "I work for the money." Another may tell you, "I work for prestige. My job serves as a stepping-stone to continually higher and more influential positions in the world." You may also find someone who labors hard and earnestly to build a better society, to remedy some social ill, or to relieve human suffering. Examine them closely; you'll find Babylon in every world-centered motivation.

What should move God's man back to his ordinary job day after day? Money? Fame? An attempt to build a paradise on this earth? Jesus gave a clear answer: "But seek first His [God's] Kingdom, and His righteousness; and all these things shall be added to you" (Matthew 6: 33). In our work, as in every other area of life, we are to serve at the pleasure of the King, not at our own pleasure. Our King has a problem on this planet. Though His will is done in heaven, it is seldom done here on earth. He is recruiting men and women who will allow His righteous will to rule them as they live and work on earth. When He finds them, the King places them strategically here and there throughout the whole world according to His own design.

Babylon and all it represents is abominable in the sight

of God (Revelation 17: 4, 5). Yet He has dared to send His chosen people into the midst of all this uncleanness. Incredible as it may seem to human logic, God does assign most of His people to ordinary employments as His first choice for their lives. One of Paul's reasons for engaging in a trade was "in order to offer ourselves as a model for you, that you might follow our example" (2 Thessalonians 3: 9).

Each of us must rely upon the Holy Spirit in discerning God's calling for us personally. If God wants you fully occupied in some form of gospel work, obey Him. If His call to you is ordinary work, obey Him just as heartily. Engagement in gospel work is no indicator of the level of one's commitment to Christ. God sets some apart for the work of the gospel, and He sets others apart to bear fruit in the ordinary vocations.

For those of us who may have been troubled by feeling that our everyday jobs are not worthy of God's Kingdom, the life of Daniel offers much encouragement. Daniel's government job came about through an outworking of circumstances. Yet he did not attempt to increase his standing before God by getting into more spiritual work. Daniel had never read Paul's letter to the Church at Corinth, yet his conduct was consistent with the command that "everybody must continue to live in the station which the Lord assigned to him . . ." (1 Corinthians 7: 17, *Williams*).

Daniel's assignment was Babylon. And there he stayed.

3

UP ON THE LAMPSTAND

WHY HAS GOD LEFT US on this earth? What are His purposes in placing us in the Babylon system of the world? In attempting to understand God's purposes it is often helpful to review our beginnings.

When Adam and Eve sinned, their action caused great loss. Usually we think first of the loss to Adam and Eve and to ourselves. We suffered broken fellowship with God and found ourselves hiding from Him. As a result our lives were cursed with pain and difficulty, and we were cut off from the eternal life of God. Being human, we are naturally most concerned about the tragedy of human loss resulting from disobedience.

It is easy for us to overlook the fact that God lost something too. And because He is God, His loss is far more tragic than ours. What did God lose? He lost the honor and praise rightfully due to Him as Creator of all that is. Our race, "even though they knew God, they did not honor Him as God, or give thanks; but they became futile in their speculations, and their foolish heart was darkened. For they exchanged the truth of God for a lie, and worshiped and served the creature rather than the Creator . . ." (Romans 1: 21, 25). Even though God had performed the supreme creative act, no one gave Him credit for it.

In ordinary human society it is unthinkable not to give credit for creative acts. If an architect designs a great building, he is given credit—perhaps with a bronze plaque inscribed with his name. Most of us have seen the credit lines at the end of television programs naming those responsible for writing or producing the shows, designing the costumes, or composing the music. If a person attaches his own name to a book written and copyrighted by another author, he violates the law and is subject to penalty. To attribute falsely the work of one person to another robs the first person of the honor rightfully belonging to him.

When sin entered the world, it robbed the Author of the universe in just this way. Scripture likens man's sinful state to darkness. Even though it ought to have been perfectly clear that God created the heavens and the earth, we have missed it. Something as basic as this must be pointed out to us. That's why the opening lines of the Bible read, "In the beginning, God created the heavens and the earth." Sin so darkened our natural minds and hearts that we could no longer honor God for His magnificent creation. As a result, men set up wooden, stone, or metal images and worshiped them as gods. They have worshiped the sun, moon, or stars. They have become enslaved by the false gods of money, sex, pleasure, or reputation. Or, like Nebuchadnezzar, they have worshiped themselves, claiming to be "self-made men" and attributing all their greatness and power to their own efforts.

God's "copyright" was stamped on everything He made. But the darkness in our hearts made us blind and deaf to the message of His handiwork. So sin robbed God of glory, honor, and praise. The wonder and admiration of men has been directed toward the made things, not toward the Maker of them. And in this God has suffered more loss than we can possibly ever know. Man lost, and lost greatly, when sin entered the world through his disobedience. But how much more did God, the infinite Creator, lose when men's hearts and minds became so darkened that no one recognized Him as the Source of all.

Thus when God looks upon the Babylon system of this world, He sees darkness—utter moral and spiritual darkness. Scripture speaks of the "domain of darkness," and tells us that our struggle is against the "world-forces of this darkness." We read that the earth's inhabitants "loved darkness." Loving darkness is totally contrary to God's very being, for we know that "God is light, and in Him there is no darkness at all" (1 John 1: 5). By enticing men into sin, Satan successfully shut out the light of the Creator so that men groped in darkness. The basic problem, then, was this: How could God beam His light back into the world following the blackout caused by sin?

There was a way. It was a costly way, but because He loves this race of men, God took it. He sent light into the world in the person of Jesus Christ, His Son. When Jesus entered the world, He fulfilled Isaiah's prophecy which said: "The people who walk in darkness will see a great light" (Isaiah 9: 2). Of Himself Jesus said, "While I am in the world, I am the light of the world" (John 9: 5).

But after paying the price of His own death to cancel sin's death-dealing power, Jesus rose again and ascended to rejoin His Father in heaven. Did His departure leave the world in darkness again? What happened when the Light of the World left the world? As we might expect, God had a plan to maintain light in the world even after Jesus returned to heaven. In one of those almost incredible statements, Jesus told His followers: "*You* are the light of the world" (Matthew 5: 14). The awesome fact is that just "as He is, so also are we in this world" (1 John 4: 17). As members of Christ's very Body, we are what He is.

In Jesus, God had a light. In Jesus' followers—those in

whom the life of Jesus abides—God has many lighted ones, because Jesus' "life was the light of men" (John 1: 4). Light by its very nature overcomes darkness. We are further told that "the light continues to shine in the darkness, for the darkness has never overpowered it" (verse 5, *Williams*). Through us, God's lighted ones, the Light of the World continues to overcome the darkness.

From practical experience we know that a light must be properly positioned if it is to illuminate the area surrounding it. A light is not enough in itself; it needs a fixture to hold it steady and in the right place. A living-room lamp may rest on an end table. In the dining room, a ceiling fixture holds the light. Streetlights are positioned on poles.

In a similar way God must position us correctly if we are to function as lights in the world. He must place us in full view. This is clear from Jesus' teaching on the subject: "You are the light of the world," He said. "A city set on a hill cannot be hidden. Nor do men light a lamp, and put it under the peck-measure, but on the lampstand; and it gives light to all who are in the house" (Matthew 5: 14, 15). Visibility is vital here. Of what use is a lamp in a closet? Lamps are not made to be concealed. They are to be so positioned that light may flood the darkness surrounding them.

God wants to use our ordinary jobs as lampstands, light fixtures. Our work stations place us in positions of visibility. If God were to cluster all His lighted ones together in clean and shining places, such an arrangement might be pleasant, but the darkness would remain. Who needs a yard light in the daytime? No, God does not want His people to huddle together away from the darkness. He wants us to be lights in the darkness. He sees us as "children of God above reproach in the midst of a crooked and perverse generation, among whom you appear as lights in the world" (Philippians 2: 15). Who could be more *in the midst* of a crooked and perverse generation than a man at work in the world?

How do we, as lights in the darkness, help solve God's original problem? When sin entered, God lost recognition, admiration, praise, thanksgiving—all the heart attitudes that rightfully belong only to Him. How do we, in our world of work, gain back for God His due? Jesus explained it in this way: "Let your light shine before men in such a way that they may see your good works, and glorify your Father who is in heaven" (Matthew 5: 16). Jesus said people will see His light when they see our good works. With what result? That men may give glory to the Father in heaven. In the original creation, God became the first One to do good works. He worked the first six days, and each work was "good" to Him. But sin blinded the eyes of men to God's original good works. He did not receive the glory due Him. Something more was needed. Since sin had darkened the old creation, a new creation was called for. "For we are His workmanship, created in Christ Jesus *for good works,* which God prepared beforehand, that we should walk in them" (Ephesians 2: 10).

Dark-hearted men will not praise God nor give Him the glory for His first good works—the sun, moon, stars, and all the other wonders of nature. So now God is doing His good works right in the midst of them through the lights He has positioned in the world. People may avoid lifting their eyes to the hills or stars to see there the glory of God, but they cannot avoid a "lighted one" working next to them hour after hour, day after day.

The book of Daniel illustrates this in an experience shared by the three godly friends of Daniel—also employees of the Babylonian government. Nebuchadnezzar made an image of gold and commanded his subjects to bow and worship it. Shadrach, Meshach, and Abed-nego refused. They were thrown into a blazing furnace, there to be joined by a fourth Figure among them who delivered them from the furnace unharmed.

Their good work (i.e., trusting God and refusing to worship an earthly, created thing) issued in praise to God from the mouth of the pagan king: "Blessed be the God of Shadrach, Meshach, and Abed-nego, who has sent His angel and delivered His servants who put their trust in Him . . . there is no other god who is able to deliver in this way" (Daniel 3: 28, 29).

In our ordinary jobs our good works can be done to the praise of God's glory. Even unbelieving co-workers will be forced to recognize that these works are not of ourselves. The world has its motives, its standards, its methods of operation. Those who are of the world recognize that which is worldly. But the good works of the Christian, originating from a heavenly Source, cannot be adequately explained in worldly terms.

Even here we must walk by faith, not by what we see. We may seldom see or hear anyone around us praising God because of our good works. But if we continue to abide in Christ, we may trust Him to store up our good works for the *future* praise of the Father. "Beloved, I urge you as aliens and strangers to abstain from fleshly lusts, which wage war against the soul. Keep your behavior excellent among the Gentiles, so that in the thing in which they slander you as evildoers, they may on account of your good deeds, as they observe them, glorify God in the day of visitation" (1 Peter 2: 11, 12). The praise God wins for Himself through us may have to wait until His final judgment. But in that day we know "that at the name of Jesus every knee should bow, of those who are in heaven, and on earth, and under the earth, and that every tongue should confess that Jesus Christ is Lord, to the glory of God the Father" (Philippians 2: 10, 11).

When a man who works in the darkness of Babylon sheds light among his fellow employees through his good works, it brings gain to God and loss to Satan. One day, praise God, even this accuser, our enemy, will be over-powered by the Light. Even He will be forced to acknowledge that "Jesus Christ is Lord, to the glory of God the Father."

In the end God will have recovered what He lost. He will be rightfully praised for creating all that exists. John, in the book of Revelation, offers us a glimpse of how it will be then. He shows us the twenty-four elders falling down before the throne of God in worship and saying: "Worthy art Thou, our Lord and our God, to receive glory and honor and power; for Thou didst create all things, and because of Thy will they existed, and were created" (Revelation 4: 11). What a privilege we have by being placed in ordinary labor. Every daily task is sacred; each one can be claimed for God to gain back the praise and glory belonging to His Name!

4

THE DAILY GRIND

IT IS NATURAL AND RIGHT, when we see the great needs of others who work near us, to want God to use us in helping to meet those needs. Yet in our eagerness to be used by God we sometimes overlook one of His basic reasons for positioning us in our particular occupation. Most of us would like to think we're "a light to those who are in darkness" (Romans 2: 19) now that we belong to God. But God sees us as we are. He knows that, even though we have turned from sin to follow Christ, much work must be done in us before we can serve as consistent channels of light.

All Christians are lights in the world. But light comes in varying degrees of brightness. A 15-watt bulb produces light, but leaves much to be desired in a reading lamp. Scripture tells us that God is always looking for enlargement and increase within the individual Christian. He does not stop working with a fruit-producing branch. Instead, He prunes it to obtain even more fruit (John 15: 2). And so it is with light. God loves the 15-watt Christian, but will always be working to increase his output of light. By what process can the light within us become brighter? In the first chapter of John we saw that Christ's "life was the light of men." It follows, then, that any increase in light will require an increase of the life of Christ within us.

Our daily work serves as one of God's major tools for cultivating and nurturing the life of Christ within us. While we may be eager to have our work used in changing the lives of others, God is eager first to change our own lives through our work. After that is under way perhaps He can use our work in the lives of others (Matthew 7: 5). How is it that an ordinary job can be used to increase the life and light of Christ in us?

A visit to the garden will help us to understand how our work can be used in this way. Before a garden is planted, the soil is full of weed seed. No one worries much if weeds grow on a barren patch of ground. But once good seed has been planted, weeds become a problem. They hinder the growth of the good plants, robbing them of sunlight, water, and food. Any increase in vegetable plant life requires a decrease in weed life. More simply stated: No hoe, no harvest.

When God begins tilling our heart-gardens, He knows full well about the weed seed—the sinful self-life which we inherited from Adam. And He knows what a hindrance the sinful self-life is to the increase of Christ's life within us. God's "hoe" is the Cross of Jesus Christ, by which we are to die to this self-life (Romans 6:1–11). Unless we are willing to keep on dying to this self-life (the "flesh" in scriptural terms), we will not see an increase of the Christ-life within us. The self-life and the Christ-life cannot peacefully coexist within the same body. Either increases only at the expense of the other (Romans 8: 13).

Through our daily work God brings into our lives circumstances which force us to choose between life and death to this self-life. Those same circumstances become opportunities for an increase of Christ's life in us, provided we choose death to the self-life. One of Daniel's on-the-job experiences illustrates this. Daniel's co-workers wanted to undermine his chances for promotion. They decided

their only avenue of attack had to be through his devotion to God. They persuaded the king to sign a decree forbidding prayer to any god other than himself for a period of thirty days, and then sat back to catch Daniel in their legal trap. When they found him praying, they reported it to the king, demanding the death penalty. Having no choice, the king ordered Daniel thrown to the lions. But God delivered Daniel, and he came to no harm.

Although Daniel escaped with his physical life, it is clear that this attack by his enemies called for death to his self-life. There is no reason to doubt that Daniel, had he chosen to, could have attempted to use his influence with King Darius to "get back" at his enemies. Yet nowhere in Scripture do we read of such a reaction. Daniel put to death the urge toward selfish vengeance that lurked in his flesh. Instead of trying to save himself, he exhibited the life of Christ, who "kept entrusting Himself to Him who judges righteously" (1 Peter 2: 23). As a result, he saw God act in his behalf—something that could not help but produce more life within Daniel. "So Daniel was taken up out of the den, and no injury whatever was found on him, because he had trusted in his God" (Daniel 6: 23).

God seeks to continue this same process in us through our experiences on the job. As we die to the self-life, the life of Christ increases within us. Take a man away from his occupation, and you remove him from a rich source of experiences in which he may count himself dead to sin (in Christ's death) and alive to God's righteousness (in Christ's resurrection life).

For men, certain women who work can become another source of potential defeat or victory over sin. Joseph's work confronted him with a problem in this area when his employer's wife tried to seduce him. Joseph refused. "How then could I do this great evil, and sin against God?" he asked her (Genesis 39: 9). The Scriptures give no

indication that Joseph did not find this woman attractive. He was a male, made of flesh and blood. Yet in counting such an act as sin against God, Joseph died to the sinful desires of his self-life.

We should trust God and thus allow Him to cause the Cross of Christ to do its mighty death-work in us. Then we will be able to obey the command to "consider the members of your earthly body as dead to immorality, impurity, passion, evil desire, and greed, which amounts to idolatry" (Colossians 3: 5). And considering ourselves dead to sin we will find ourselves "alive to God in Christ Jesus" (Romans 6: 11). The life of Jesus is the light of men. As His life increases, so will the light within, and we will be able to say with David: "For Thou dost light my lamp; the Lord my God illumines my darkness" (Psalm 18: 28).

Once the light within us has brightened considerably, we might naturally assume it will automatically begin to stream forth to those around us. Many times, however, this does not happen and we wonder why. Scripture reveals the reason. In 2 Corinthians 4: 6, Paul writes of the light which God has caused to shine within us. Then he calls this light a treasure, pointing out that we "have this treasure in earthen vessels" (v. 7). The picture drawn for us is clear: we Christians are like earthen jars containing the light of Jesus Christ.

A striking parallel to this picture is seen in the Old Testament account of Gideon. Each of Gideon's 300 warriors carried a lighted torch inside an empty jar. Because the jars effectively blocked the light, Gideon's men were able to move right to the outskirts of the enemy camp. Even the sentries did not see the lights. Then suddenly each man blew his trumpet and broke his empty jar. The light flooded the darkness and the battle was won (Judges 7: 16–22).

Our "earthen vessels," like Gideon's jars, can hide the

light within. The light is there, all right, but little of it escapes to the outside. Jesus, knowing this would be a problem, told us not to hide the light in some enclosed container, but to let it shine out to light the way for those near us (Matthew 5: 15, 16). How, then, can the light within shine out if our "earthen vessels" shut it in? Gideon's army knew. The earthen vessels must be broken. Our outward beings, our "containers," must be broken if the inner light is to shine through.

There are two important differences between our own earthen jars and those used by Gideon's men. First, Gideon's warriors had no future use for their broken jars. Once broken, the jars were worthless to them. God, however, wants His treasure to continue in the earthenware pot with all its weaknesses. God does not break us to throw us away—instead, He breaks us for increased use, so that His life and light can better flow through us.

The second important difference is that Gideon's jars were easily broken, perhaps even carelessly broken. One blow and the jars scattered into fragments. But when God breaks us, He does it carefully, purposefully. Our lives need not one blow, but many blows. And these take time and a variety of circumstances, thus making our occupation an ideal tool for God to use in the breaking process. We spend a great deal of time at work. We encounter an endless variety of situations on the job. What better setup could be devised for God's breaking procedure?

Joseph's career offers several good examples of how God uses job situations to break us. The first blow came while on an assignment from his father, Jacob. Seventeen-year-old Joseph had been sent to see how his brothers were faring with the family flocks some distance from home. He obeyed, but his brothers sold him to some traders, who in turn took him to Egypt and sold him to Potiphar. What a blow! Joseph's right conduct was rewarded by his being sold into slavery by his own flesh and blood. Another blow came when Joseph honored God in refusing to sin with Potiphar's wife. She lied about the whole incident, turning it around to make it appear as if Joseph had propositioned her. As a result, Potiphar threw Joseph into prison.

Although Joseph knew this imprisonment was undeserved, he did not give in to bitterness. Continuing in fellowship with God, he was given success even in prison. Joseph so impressed the keeper of the prison that he was put in charge of all the other prisoners. Though neither bitter nor impatient, Joseph still wanted out. On one occasion the king's butler, a fellow prisoner, asked Joseph to interpret a dream. God gave Joseph the interpretation: the butler would be released and restored to his former post in three days. Then Joseph asked the butler to inform Pharaoh of his plight and to set him free.

A third blow came when the butler forgot all about Joseph. For two more years Joseph remained in the prison, unrewarded for the kindness he had shown to the butler. But when Pharaoh had a dream which none of the wise men could interpret, the butler's memory suddenly improved. He told Pharaoh how Joseph had accurately interpreted his dream while in prison. Accordingly, Joseph was summoned. God gave him the interpretation of Pharaoh's dream. A famine was to come upon the whole land, but Joseph offered a plan to avert starvation for the people, including a suggestion that Pharaoh appoint a man to oversee a program of stockpiling reserves.

Joseph was now thirty. Thirteen years had passed since the first blow had fallen. But in those years, God had broken him so that light was evident in his life. Even Pharaoh, the pagan ruler of Egypt, recognized it. He said to his servants, "Can we find a man like this, in whom is a divine spirit?" And to Joseph he said, "Since God has informed you of all this, there is no one so discerning and wise as you are. You shall be over my house, and according to your command all my people shall do homage; only in the throne I will be greater than you . . . . See I have set you over all the land of Egypt" (Genesis 41: 38–41).

Those thirteen years were costly. The blows were no more pleasant to Joseph than they would have been to any of us. He named his first son Manasseh, saying, "God has made me forget all my trouble and all my father's household." And his second son he called Ephraim, for he said, "God has made me fruitful in the land of my affliction" (Genesis 41: 51, 52). Trouble, affliction. These were Joseph's words to describe the thirteen years. Yet in all these blows he recognized the hand of God. He later told his brothers who had sold him into slavery, thereby opening the door to all his troubles: ". . . it was not you who sent me here, but God" (Genesis 45: 8).

How ready are we to acknowledge the hand of God in the reversals which occur on the job? Someone else gets that promotion to a position we know we deserve. Our good work goes unrecognized, unappreciated. Perhaps our best efforts are cut to shreds by criticism. A raise in salary fails to materialize, or we get transferred to an undesirable location. These things hurt—but praise God for every one of them! Why? Because He has placed us in our jobs for a purpose, and a part of this purpose is to break us so that we may become channels for His light, not mere containers of it. We are not wise enough even to know how to break our outward selves. And we would lack the courage to strike the blow even if we knew how. But our God knows, and in love He brings the hammer against us in just the right places and at just the right times. We may have called adverse circumstances "the breaks," little realizing what an apt description that is of what God is seeking to do in us.

There is another aspect of God's dealing in our work lives which relates to this whole process of creating life and light in us and releasing it through us. This is the matter of testing. From the beginning God has tested His people. When He placed Adam and Eve in the Garden of Eden, He included a test—a forbidden tree. They failed the test, but through it the secret desires of their inner hearts became apparent.

Through Moses God told the Israelites to expect testing: "If a prophet or a dreamer of dreams arises among you and gives you a sign or a wonder, and the sign or the wonder comes true, concerning which he spoke to you, saying, 'Let us go after other gods (whom you have not known) and let us serve them,' you shall not listen to the words of that prophet or that dreamer of dreams; for the Lord your God is testing you to find out if you love the Lord your God with all your heart and with all your soul" (Deuteronomy 13: 1–3).

As God forms Christ within us, He tests and tries us to be certain that the material measures up and that the work is being done thoroughly. Peter tells us that these trials and tests come "that the proof of your faith, being more precious than gold which is perishable, even though tested by fire, may be found to result in praise and glory and honor at the revelation of Jesus Christ" (1 Peter 1: 7).

This testing goes beyond merely demonstrating our faith before men. An audience is watching us from the realms of heaven. Job, an upright and blameless resident of Uz, worshiped God wholeheartedly. Yet Satan doubted that Job was really as wholehearted toward God as he appeared. "Test him," Satan said in effect to God. How? ". . . put forth Thy hand now and touch all that he has; he will surely curse Thee to Thy face" (Job 1: 11). So the Lord allowed Satan to ruin everything except Job himself. Still Job did not change his heart attitude toward God. Satan came before God again, asking for a more severe test: ". . . touch his bone and his flesh; he will curse Thee to Thy face" (2: 5).

Job's ultimate triumph through this test proved that his faith in God was of pure metal. He had said that God "knows the way I take; when He has tried me, I shall come forth as gold" (23: 10). And gold he proved to be. Then Satan was forced to acknowledge that in Job God had a man whose faith was real, whose heart and soul loved God more than his own life. Our audience is not only the world of men. God is proving His sovereignty in the heavenly places. And He is using us to prove it.

Large automobile manufacturers maintain extensive testing grounds. On these elaborate courses their vehicles must prove themselves reliable under every adverse condition. Our occupations are often used by God as testing grounds. What attachments really hold our hearts? Does God enjoy the supreme allegiance there? Or do the things of this world and our own bodies mean more to us? Through the adverse circumstances God allows on the job, the answer to these questions will become clear.

Temptations to sin should be recognized as tests. Jesus taught us to pray that God would not lead us into temptation. We should not be out seeking these testings. Yet we should receive them thankfully when they come. It was the Holy Spirit of God who led Jesus into the wilderness to be tempted. Satan did the tempting, not God. Yet it was God who led His Son into the place of testing. Likewise, in our daily work the Lord will sometimes lead us into situations where Satan can tempt us. Our response will indicate to God, to Satan, to ourselves, and sometimes to others what really lies in our hearts. Thank God we have His promise that He "will not allow you to be tempted beyond what you are able; but with the temptation will provide the way of escape also, that you may be able to endure it" (1

Corinthians 10: 13).

How shall we view the "daily grind"? Perhaps we can compare it to the grinding of a lens. God wants to focus the Light of the World through us and beam it into this world's darkness. But first He must shape the glass into an effective lens. Our work can, if we allow it and recognize God's hand in it, be used to grind us, smooth us, polish us, and fit us for the service of the living God. Through the commonplace and humdrum circumstances of every day, we are given opportunity to die to self and live for Christ alone. We are broken, and we are tested. In it all, God wants to increase His light within us, then through us to concentrate His healing rays on others who live and work in Babylon.

5

TRIMMING THE LAMPS

GOD'S WORK IN US is never meant to build only ourselves; He also intends to build others through us. Who
are these others? Paul wrote, "while we have opportunity,
let us do good to all men, and especially to those who are of
the household of the faith" (Galatians 6: 10). All people
are included in the "others" God wants to bless through
us. But the word "especially" introduces a priority. We
owe our ministry of love and light to everyone, but one
group is to be given special attention, namely fellow members of the household of the faith. First God's people, then
the world. This is consistently God's order of blessing men
throughout the Scripture record.

All true believers in Christ are included in the household of the faith. This means that in the place where I work
the houseold of the faith is made up of all the saints to be
found there. It may also mean that my responsibility ex-
tends to many more Christians than I had previously im-
agined.

This household of the faith in my work community may
include those who are weak in faith (Romans 14: 1), those
who feel they cannot eat certain things (v. 2), or those who
have different ideas on which day ought to be set apart for
worship (v. 5). It may include both spiritual and carnal
Christians (1 Corinthians 3: 1)—well-taught, untaught, or

even wrongly taught Christians (1 Corinthians 15: 12). The one common link between these varied members of God's household is simply this: they have found their way into fellowship with God through trusting Jesus Christ.

Christ brings life and light into the lives of believers. In His light we make a wonderful discovery: not only do we enjoy fellowship with God, but also with every other Christian. Scripture promises that "if we walk in the light as He Himself is in the light, we have fellowship *with one another* . . ." (1 John 1: 7). This household of the faith is to be a household of fellowship, a close-knit, caring community of Christians. Members of this household are not committed to one another because they share similar views on certain pet doctrines. Their ties are not based on membership in the same earth-based organization. Nor is their fellowship based on the fact that they may worship in the same building on Sundays. Rather, the members of this household share a common life in the family of God. They experience this fellowship, not by signing a membership list but by simply walking in God's light.

A question comes quickly to mind: How do we recognize God's household? It cannot be seen simply with our physical eyes. Spiritual sight is needed here. God's household is so large we can never capture or contain it. A certain restaurant advertises that its view of a waterfall is so delightful the management may bottle it. But bottling a waterfall would only ruin the view. So it is with the Church. We can only recognize and serve it when we meet it. We can't bottle it up to serve it at our own convenience. Spiritual sight will recognize the Church where it encounters the Spirit of Christ in another believer or group of believers. Jesus left us no list of "approved" organizations by which we may discern the true believers. He left us only one simple test: fruit. Psalm 1 compares the man of God to a tree which bears its fruit in season. Jesus said that a "tree is known by its fruit" (Matthew 12: 33).

What is fruit? Fruit is that which results from the life within a tree. It is produced for others, not for the tree itself. Fruit is desirable, and satisfies hunger. Fruit is full of seed which, if planted, can produce more fruit. Spiritual fruit results from Christ's life within a Christian. It is produced first to please God, and then to bless others. Spiritual fruit is attractive to hungry hearts. And those who eat it will discover at its core some seeds like that which produced it.

John the Baptist urged the people who came to him for baptism to "bring forth fruits in keeping with your repentance" (Luke 3: 8). They asked him to be more specific. He told them to share with the needy, to be honest in their dealings, to be fair, and to be content with what they had—all of which are products of the life of God. In Ephesians 5: 9 we read that "the fruit of the light consists in all goodness and righteousness and truth." Praise and thanksgiving to God are fruits of the lips (Hebrews 13: 15). Good works are fruit in the life of a Christian (Colossians 1: 10). The well-known list in Galatians 5: 22, 23 adds much to our understanding of spiritual fruit: love, joy, peace, patience, kindness, goodness, faithfulness, gentleness, self-control.

These, then, are among the fruits that will enable us to recognize other members of Christ's Body. We may have to place less reliance upon some of our previous techniques for discovering fellow Christians. Perhaps we have looked for a label. If a man called himself "evangelical," this may have been convincing enough for us. We may have looked for a cross worn on the lapel or a Bible on the shelf. But we ought to be careful. The Pharisees had all these outward signs. The very name Pharisee meant "separated." They wore phylacteries containing Scripture portions on their foreheads and upper arms. Their robes displayed extra-long tassels to underscore their spiritual stature. They enjoyed high positions and awesome ecclesiastical titles. They had an impressive display of religion, but no fruit. Today, too, we must be careful to recognize our Christian brothers and sisters in the way Jesus appointed—by their fruit. Any other measurement will mislead us, because we know that many who say "Lord, Lord" will never enter His Kingdom.

Once we've identified other Christians in the shop or office, how can we serve them? There are no Sunday school classrooms in our work places. We can't take job time for prayer meetings. Pulpits and pews have no place in the job setting. In this age of supersized organizations we too readily assume that service must be programmed to be effective. But there is a notable lack of "programming" (in the modern sense of this term) in Scripture. A believer in New Testament times who wanted to serve others did not wait until he had credentials in the right organization. In love, he simply used whatever gift he had and ministered with it.

Two examples from the life of Daniel may help us to understand how an unprogrammed event can be turned into ministry. Shortly after arriving in Babylon, Daniel and his friends, Shadrach, Meshach, and Abed-nego, were assigned food from the royal menu. They could not eat such food in good conscience. Daniel went to their supervisor and asked that all four of them be excused from the regular diet and be fed only vegetables and water. In one spirit, these four underwent the test diet for ten days. At the end of that time, God granted them better health than all the others in the royal court. They had gone through a test together, and had triumphed. How this must have cemented the bond of love between them!

This was a very "non-programmed" event. A situation had come up on the job. Four of God's people stood shoulder to shoulder to meet this trial to their faith. With what result? The faith of this foursome "overcame the world"; they were allowed to continue on a diet that would not defile them. There was no need for preplanning, committee meetings, or parliamentary procedures. Conditions on the job simply offered an opportunity for a ministry of strengthening and encouraging one another.

When Nebuchadnezzar was troubled by a dream which no one could repeat or interpret, he ordered a purge of all his wise men, including Daniel and his three friends. Again, the job had brought along a difficult set of circumstances. Daniel met with his friends, they prayed, and their prayers were answered. God revealed the dream and its interpretation to Daniel. He related it all to the king, and their lives were spared. All this came about simply because a small handful of godly men met the circumstances of their routine work in faith. Their prayer meeting was not programmed, but God answered mightily.

No list, however complete, could fully encompass the various forms of service that we may be called upon to render to our fellow Christians. This is because all true work for our brothers originates in what God is doing for them. Jesus Himself only did the works He saw His Father doing. God's work on our behalf covers the whole gamut of our need—physical, mental, emotional, social, spiritual. Therefore, within the varied members of the Body of Christ we should expect to find wide-ranging ministries. Some ministries will be outward, some hidden. Some spectacular, some routine. Your ministry and mine may be completely unalike. This should cause us to thank God who has included such a rich diversity of gifts and ministries within Christ's Body. What are some of the different forms that service may take on the job?

Before everything else, love must rule us. How are Christians to love? The general law of love is: "Love your neighbor in the way you love yourself." We owe this much love to all men, believer and unbeliever. But Jesus gave us an additional measurement concerning love for our fellow believers. He said: "Just as the Father has loved Me, I have also loved you . . . . This is My commandment, that you love one another, just as I have loved you" (John 15: 9, 12). Jesus commands us to love each other in the same way He loves us. How does He love us? Just as the Father loves Him!

When Jesus spoke of love, He did not mean only sentiment and a passing emotion. He spoke of a strong, self-giving love. "For God so loved the world, that He *gave* . . . ." Just as the Father loved, so did the Son, who "did not come to be served, but to serve, and to *give* His life a ransom for many" (Matthew 20: 28). Love like this would never have been known in the world had Christ not revealed it. "We know love by this, that He laid down His life for us; and we ought to lay down our lives for the brethren" (1 John 3: 16).

Self-giving love is neither theoretical nor abstract. It operates in specific life situations. No program is needed to supply love with opportunities to serve. Scripture tells us to do good "as opportunity offers" (Galatians 6: 10, *Phillips*). Life brings along the opportunities, and life on the job is no exception. Love recognizes these opportunities and acts accordingly.

Suppose a Christian brother, through carelessness, commits a blunder which ruins a whole month's work on a project which I've headed. The whole crew is down on him, even though he's admitted his error and would undo the damage if that were possible. At the moment his greatest need is for wholehearted forgiveness. Life has provided me with an opportunity to serve my Christian brother. Will I? Or will my disappointment in the spoiled effort cause me to forgive half-heartedly? Forgiving is one service none of us can neglect lightly. "For if you forgive men for their transgressions, your heavenly Father will also forgive you," Jesus said. "But if you do not forgive men, then your Father will not forgive your transgressions" (Matthew 6: 14, 15). If we would do the work of God, we must be in the forgiving business. He is.

We who work can serve by listening. But someone may object: "I can't spend job time listening to someone carry on about their problems—I'd never get my work done!" Would we be willing to give up coffee breaks or noon hours in this ministry if the Lord were to open the opportunity? Serving by listening, however, is not limited to private counseling sessions. How carefully do we listen to others in work-oriented conversations? Are we able to discern spiritual conditions in other Christians while they talk about very ordinary matters? Are they given to complaining? This should tell us something about their inner needs. Do trifles upset others, causing them to lose patience? Does their speech convey contentment? Gratitude? Greed? Inner peace? Resentment? An unforgiving spirit? Each time a brother opens his mouth to speak there is an opportunity to perceive something of his real need. Scripture says, "But let every one be quick to hear, slow to speak . . ." (James 1: 19). Again, this ministry is only an extension of God's working. One of the most reassuring truths of the Bible is that when we speak, God hears. We who serve the God who listens should also listen to one another.

The ministry of listening should lead into the ministry of prayer. When, by listening, we begin to understand our brother's need, we can pray for him more effectively. Interceding for God's other children is a privilege. Not everyone was given this ministry in the Old Testament. In the main, it was the place of the priest to go before God on behalf of others. But today we can approach the throne of

God directly through Christ, not only for ourselves, but also for others. In this way we carry out our function as the "holy priesthood" of New Testament believers. Do we care enough about our brothers at work to spend off-job time praying for them? We will if we look to Jesus and do only what we see Him doing.

Closely linked with the ministry of prayer is that of bringing back the strays. We who hold ordinary jobs may have a greater opportunity and responsibility in this ministry than those in gospel work. Without much effort a person can keep up good appearances on Sunday in front of the church-going crowd. But how does he live during the week? What is his reputation on the job and with the general public? A professional pastor has limited opportunity to observe his brothers and sisters in their "natural habitats."

The working man, however, may have up to eight hours a day, five days a week to see his brother as he actually is. Two-facedness will show in the everyday dealings with people. A bad temper, dishonesty, idle gossip, greed—all these become apparent on the job. Thus, we are responsible when it becomes necessary to serve our fellow Christians with words of correction, reproof, or instruction. "My brethren," James wrote, "if any among you strays from the truth, and one turns him back; let him know that he who turns a sinner from the error of his way will save his soul from death, and will cover a multitude of sins" (James 5: 19, 20). This is a fragile ministry, one which must be carefully packaged in love and prayer. And like all other service, bringing back those who stray is simply carrying on what God has been doing for ages.

Perhaps there would be less straying from the truth if God's people faithfully served each other with encouragement. Before sin gets a grip on the life of a believer, there is usually a period of struggle. In every time of testing, Scripture tells us, God provides a way of escape. But if our resistance is low we may miss seeing that way of escape. Sometimes it takes a fellow believer to serve us with a word of encouragement. As Scripture says: "Take care, brethren, lest there should be in any one of you an evil, unbelieving heart, in falling away from the living God. But *encourage* one another day after day, as long as it is still called 'Today,' lest any one of you be hardened by the deceitfulness of sin" (Hebrews 3: 12, 13).

The word here translated "encourage" is another form of the word used as a name for the Holy Spirit, the "Comforter." Again, it is clear that our work for our brothers and sisters in Christ is to be exactly the same work in which our triune God engages Himself. God lifts up the weary, comforts those with breaking hearts, and supports the weak. He longs that you and I, in experiencing His encouragement in our own lives, will "consider how to stimulate one another to love and good deeds . . . *encouraging* one another; and all the more, as you see the day drawing near" (Hebrews 10: 24, 25).

Yet another service is that of setting an example. A good example can serve as unspoken encouragement to continue in the Way. Frequently the quiet consistency of a life lived in union with Christ carries a more convincing message than any sermon. It is not surprising that God has emphasized in the Scriptures this need for example-setting.

Jesus Himself served others by setting an example. "Christ also suffered for you, leaving you an example for you to follow in His steps" (1 Peter 2: 21). Paul urged the Philippian believers to "join in following my example, and observe those who walk according to the pattern you have in us" (Philippians 3: 17). Elders, in shepherding local churches, are to be "examples to the flock" (1 Peter 5: 3).

Sermons and books often contain illustrations from the

lives of famous Christians in gospel work. These have a place. But how great is the need for living examples of the Christian faith in the everyday work place! If God has assigned me to work in an office, I need the examples of others who also work there. Just seeing another brother remain faithful to Christ while undergoing trials similar to my own serves to encourage and strengthen me in my own walk with God.

These are only a few of the ministries through which God would have us serve our fellow Christians on the job. They, as well as we, are lamps in this dark world. Oil-burning lamps need daily attention to be kept in trim. Each of us, as a believer-priest, has the privilege and responsibility to "trim the lamps," just as the priests in the Old Testament trimmed the lamps which burned in the Tabernacle (Exodus 30: 7).

However large our service to others may become, we must never forget that there is also a ministry in allowing others to minister to us. Jesus came not to be served, but to serve. He served His disciples by washing their feet. Yet He allowed a woman who was less than nothing in the eyes of the Pharisees to wash His feet with her tears and anoint them with perfume. There are times when the most needed service will be that of receiving help from others. My lamp needs trimming, too. True, "it is *more* blessed to give than to receive." Yet receiving is still blessed, especially when by it we allow others to experience the "more" through their giving to us.

Loving, forgiving, listening, praying, bringing back those who stray, encouraging, setting examples, submitting to the ministry of other believers at work—none of these are "flashy" ministries. The applause will be scanty. Many organized efforts and heavily advertised special events will command far more attention, even among believers. But massive efforts are here and gone. Specially gifted speakers can move large audiences—then they move on to other crowds. After all the fanfare and banners, we are often disappointed by a lack of any lasting result.

In spite of man's appetite for the spectacular and exciting, the Light of the World still travels with real consistency and power through the ordinary believer who lives his quiet, unimpressive life in union with Christ. My common Christian brother at work may not sparkle and sizzle like the world-renowned speaker or the musician on the record jacket, but he is there when I need him. I may be impressed by someone who is here this week and gone the next, but I have no way to observe whether his faith holds him steady after the thrill of the big event has subsided.

My Christian brother may not impress me at all until one day I suddenly realize that there's an uncommon power quietly at work in this common co-worker. Then, perhaps, my eyes will begin to open to some of the on-the-job ministries God plans for me. The things I had not even thought of as ministries I now begin to see as God sees them. Serving God, I see, is not simply involvement in activities and programs over at "our" church. Rather, serving God is the sum total of a unified life, all of it sacred, continually offered up to Him.

Get reacquainted with Jesus in the Scriptures. You will come to love in a new way this humble-hearted King who came to the carpenter shop and the common folk. The old split-level life with its sacred/secular burden will drop from your shoulders as you shoulder the new and unified life which God envisions for you. Then you will understand what Jesus meant when He said, "My load is light" (Matthew 11: 30).

6

GLOWING WITHOUT GLARING

SHARING THE LIGHT OF THE WORLD with non-Christians is one more reason God has put us to work in ordinary jobs. But how do we share this light? Do we glow? Or glare?

Once, when I was in college, my roommate came home late, long after I'd gone to sleep. Suddenly I was conscious of a brilliant light in my face. Struggling to an upright position, I peered bleary-eyed through the glare of his powerful flashlight. "What are you trying to prove?" I demanded.

"Just wanted to see if you were asleep," he said.

Holding a flashlight beam on a path to light the way for a friend is one thing, but aiming the glare directly into his eyes is quite another!

In this matter of witnessing to non-Christians it is easy to swerve into one of two extremes. Some Christians feel compelled to preach Christ to unsaved co-workers whenever they can corner them. Such tactics soon create tensions and hostilities in any group of working people. Unbelievers are expert at tuning out "witnessing" of this sort.

At the opposite extreme, other Christians never open their mouths for Christ on the job. They can work in a place for years without speaking a word concerning their

Savior. Either extreme falls short of the work of evangelism which God wants to accomplish.

Strange as it may seem, both these failures in evangelism frequently occur among Christians who have been taught that "winning souls" is God's only purpose in putting them in a job. According to human logic it would seem that the way to accomplish more evangelism would be to emphasize it above all else, to teach Christians that verbal witnessing is their sole service in this world. However, in spite of so much talk about evangelism, we are too often disappointed in how little of it actually gets done.

There are reasons for this failure. When evangelism is emphasized above and beyond its scriptural proportion to other ministries, severe guilt feelings begin to grow. Christians may blame themselves for the millions who die outside of Christ. In some believers the pressure can mount to the point where they force their light to glare. Jesus simply told us to "let" it shine (Matthew 5: 16). We all need Spirit-inspired boldness to speak God's Word. But there is also a fleshly forwardness which does more harm than good.

In other believers, an out-of-proportion emphasis on evangelism can foster a guilt-ridden silence. Perhaps they have been embarrassed by the glare of their excessively vocal brothers. Thinking that this was normal witnessing, they may have recoiled from any idea of similarly forcing their faith upon non-Christians. It is true that much of our failure to witness comes from fear, from being afraid of what people may think of us. Only heaven-sent boldness can conquer such fear. But a distorted picture of evangelism can produce another kind of fear: a fear that associates witnessing with being pushy, unkind, and insensitive. That fear, too, can stop our mouths.

The New Testament writers spent comparatively few words on evangelism. Jesus told His disciples to proclaim the gospel in every nation. He promised that after the Holy Spirit had come upon them they would be witnesses. But the letters in the New Testament written to various churches do not urge believers to "get out and make converts." Instead, the emphasis is upon the relationships of the Christian, first to God through Christ and then to his fellow believer. The New Testament writers knew that when these two relationships are in order, evangelism is spontaneous.

Evangelism is important, extremely so. But when we become preoccupied with it alone, losing sight of its scriptural balance among other forms of service, we actually hinder God's plan for bringing about new spiritual births. God's method of reaching out and bringing new believers into His household of faith centers in the Church. We are not to operate as a loose collection of freelance "salesmen" working independently according to our own plans. Rather, we are to function as the corporate Body of Christ whose members work together under the direction of the Head to accomplish God's purposes.

In fact, God's first step in reaching the world doesn't directly concern the world. The seventeenth chapter of John records one of the last prayers of Jesus while on earth. From the tone of His words we know that the whole longing of His heart was being summed up to the Father. We might expect Him to pray for the salvation of those who had not received Him. Instead, we find Him praying: "I do not ask on behalf of the world . . ." (v. 9).

For His followers, Jesus asks a number of things. One request is repeated many times in various forms. He asks that His disciples might be one even as He and the Father are one (v. 11). He asks that they may all be one (v. 21). He again asks that they may be one just as He and the Father are one (v. 22). He asks that they may be "perfected in unity" (v. 23). Unity among His followers was uppermost in Jesus' heart as He prayed. Why did He ask so strongly for unity among Christians? Was the unbelieving world left totally out of Jesus' concern? Why didn't He pray for the lost?

He did pray for the world, but not directly. Blessing for the world was to come indirectly, as a result of His Father's answer to Jesus' prayer for the Church. He prayed that His followers "may all be one; even as Thou, Father, art in Me, and I in Thee, that they also may be in Us; *that the world may believe that Thou didst send Me*" (v. 21). Again in verse twenty-three He prayed that Christians "may be perfected in unity, *that the world may know that Thou didst send Me, and didst love them,* even as Thou didst love Me."

Scripture illustrates how this prayer of Jesus was answered in one specific instance. The infant church "*all with one mind* were continually devoting themselves to prayer . . ." (Acts 1: 14). In this unified condition the Church became a "leak-proof" container for the fullness of the Holy Spirit's presence and power. Peter stood up and preached on the day of Pentecost, and some 3,000 non-Christians were won for Christ. But the power wasn't centered in Peter. The power for evangelism was centered in the united members of the Body of Christ. Peter happened to be the "mouth member" on this occasion. Even after the addition of 3,000 baby Christians, we still find this church "continuing with one mind . . ." (Acts 2: 46). As the unity continued, so did the evangelism: "And the Lord was adding to their number day by day those who were being saved" (v. 47).

When will today's world know and believe? When it sees that same oneness of mind between true Christians which exists between God the Father and the Son. Jesus' prayer makes it plain that the starting point in evangelism is not better techniques or more training, but a demonstration of heaven's unity between believers on earth. Jesus did not ask anything directly for the world because the world had not received Him. His authority was not acknowledged or recognized in the world. But in the hearts of His own, He could accomplish His will and demonstrate before the world the great love of God. Here, in the unity of the Church, lies the first key to effective evangelism. "By this," Jesus had said, "all men will know that you are My disciples, if you have love for one another" (John 13: 35). Love like this does not glare. It glows with the warmth of a campfire burning and beckoning in the darkness of Babylon's coldness, division, and hostility.

The practical implications of this on the job should be obvious. My first responsibility in evangelism is to love the other Christians around me with the same love that exists between the Father and His Son Jesus. No matter how strongly our diverse backgrounds may seem to divide us, no matter how undesirable another believer may seem to be in the flesh, I am to love him—for without this unity I will hinder non-Christians from knowing and believing that Jesus was sent by God. This is easier said than practiced. Some of the "gems" among God's living stones are as yet uncut and unpolished. Many will be abrasive in attitude and action. Can I love, forgive, and serve them as Jesus does?

How perfectly various facets of our Christian lives fit into one harmonious whole! In the previous chapter we briefly examined various ministries to other Christians around us on the job. Now, in considering our witness to non-Christians, we find that our oneness with other believers undergirds our evangelism. Visible love and unity between Christians is the first step in our witness to the world. And how better can we make our unity visible than by serving one another in love?

So it is by means of Christ's Body, the Church, that God reaches out to touch the unbelieving world. When the various members of the Body demonstrate their oneness before the world, the world takes notice. Real brotherhood like this is not earthly; it cannot be explained in terms of the world. Only Christ, who came from the Father above, could be the source for unity like this. This unified Body of Christ will also speak to unbelievers through members especially gifted in evangelism and through other members as the Holy Spirit opens opportunity. Thus all members, whether through the love they exhibit or the words they speak to unbelievers, take part in this grand work of proclaiming the gospel.

How can I glow on the job without glaring? When I work with the same people day after day, the situation resembles that of a family. In family life no one appreciates nagging. Neither do people appreciate "spiritual nagging." No doubt it was with this in mind that Peter told wives to "be submissive to your own husbands so that even if any of them are disobedient to the word they may be won without a word by the behavior of their wives" (1 Peter 3: 1). A Christian wife who continually harangues her husband about his need for salvation will soon be about as welcome as a dripping faucet (Proverbs 19: 13). There is a better way, Peter said. Win that husband over by your conduct.

When we work with people in the shop or office for a time, they soon know where we stand. Our conversation will reveal it outwardly. Our conduct will also speak. We share with them what Christ has done in our lives when opportunity presents itself. But still they are not Christians. What should we do then? If we are sensitive, we will know when that nagging point is near. If, however, we are driven by the idea that making converts is our only reason for being on the job, we may be tempted to ignore the inner voice that warns "Back off!" and plunge ahead in a boldness of our own making.

Certain members of Christ's Body whose commission

calls them to travel and preach can "shake off the dust of [their] feet" if people refuse them a hearing (Matthew 10: 14; Acts 13: 51). But we who are called to everyday tasks are often confined to an office or shop. Even after unbelievers refuse us a hearing, we must continue to live and work harmoniously with them. "Spiritual nagging" will only create animosities. We are to love our non-Christian neighbors at work as we love ourselves. Love doesn't nag.

David wrote: "The heavens are telling of the glory of God; and the firmament is declaring the work of His hands. Day to day pours forth speech, and night to night reveals knowledge. *There is no speech, nor are there words; their voice is not heard*" (Psalm 19: 1–3). The heavens are making a declaration, but doing so by what they are rather than by what they say audibly. We who are members of the Body of Christ have an advantage over the heavens; we can speak audibly. But we should never forget the power of communication that lies simply in what we are.

What are some of the ways by which our lives can witness on the job? A most important matter is the respect we have for authority. Paul instructed Timothy: "Let all who are under the yoke as slaves regard their own masters as worthy of all honor so that the name of God and our doctrine may not be spoken against" (1 Timothy 6: 1). We employees are not slaves in the strict meaning of that word. Yet our employers and supervisors are "masters" over us while we are on the job. And Jesus, who has received all authority, directs us to respect even earthly authority.

Daniel is a good example of the right kind of respect for earthly authority. King Nebuchadnezzar had dreamed another dream and wanted an interpretation. As it happened, this dream concerned God's plan to deal severely with Nebuchadnezzar. Daniel found no pleasure in the interpretation he had to give. "My lord," he said to

Nebuchadnezzar, "if only the dream applied to those who hate you, and its interpretation to your adversaries!" (Daniel 4: 19). Even though Nebuchadnezzar was a pagan king whose diet and other habits repelled this man of God, Daniel respected his superior.

In the world there is a growing disrespect for authority. It is common to hear employees grumbling and complaining about the boss behind his back. There is an added danger for Christians who work for unbelieving employers, that of losing respect for them because of their lack of faith in Christ. But this is not scriptural. We are to honor those to whom honor is due, even though, by human reasoning, they may not deserve such honor. By honoring our supervisors, Scripture says, we will not allow unbelievers to use our disrespect as a means of speaking against the name of God and the Christian teaching.

Our performance on the job is another form of witness. Paul wrote: "Slaves, be obedient to those who are your masters according to the flesh, with fear and trembling, in the sincerity of your heart, as to Christ; not by way of eye-service as men-pleasers, but as slaves of Christ, doing the will of God from the heart" (Ephesians 6: 5, 6). And to the slaves in Colossae, he wrote: "Whatever you do, do your work heartily, as for the Lord rather than for men" (Colossians 3: 23).

In a small book entitled *The 'Jesus Family' in Communist China,* Dr. D. Vaughan Rees notes that the Chinese Christians "looked on labour as a sacred trust, which was to be done for God . . . . Since labour is a sacred trust, to do one's best is to add interest and zest to one's work. The sanctity of labour is sufficient incentive." Dr. Rees tells of a young Chinese man who was assigned to him as a personal valet. "He did the most menial jobs for me, jobs which I never asked of him. When I thanked him he told me straight out that being thanked rather dulled the keen edge of his service for the Lord. I gradually learned that this was not simply a gesture, but a real attitude deeply seated in his spiritual life. . . . He told me that *his work was his only method of preaching. . . .*Just after my arrival, since he had been allocated to me, I called him. He . . . came running at once. I wondered to myself, if after a few months, he would run like that. He served me all the two years I was there, and to the last day he never changed. I cannot but testify to this and glorify God for His grace in that young man."

Those of us who have been placed by God into ordinary vocations should learn how our work can be used by God to speak to the world around us. This will mean that our work will have to be of a different quality than that typical of the world. The unbeliever says: "Don't expect to get any more work out of me unless you pay me more." He says this because he is not really serving his employer, he is serving money. But the Christian who serves God in his work will not measure out his efforts in proportion to the size of his paycheck. He will serve gladly, heartily, eagerly—simply because he is serving one Employer, the Lord, and expects the Lord to reward him. What a new light this sheds on the most menial and insignificant tasks, tasks which to most men would be sheer drudgery!

There will also be times for words of witness at work. We should remember that our employers are not paying us to sermonize on company time. But a word in season is often appropriate, perhaps paving the way for more words during coffee breaks, lunch hours, or during off hours. When it comes to words, we should trust God to bring about the opportunities. Very often, opportunities to give a word of testimony come very naturally through circumstances on the job.

When the opportunity comes to open our mouths for Jesus, we should do so carefully and respectfully. Peter wrote that believers were always to be "ready to make a defense to every one who asks you to give an account for the hope that is in you, yet with gentleness and reverence" (1 Peter 3:15). It is a privilege to speak in the name of our Lord, and we ought not to treat the privilege lightly. What we say and how we say it may well have a deep and long-lasting effect upon the persons to whom we speak. Paul also gave instructions on how we are to speak to non-Christians: "Conduct yourselves with wisdom toward outsiders, making the most of the opportunity. Let your speech always be with grace, seasoned, as it were, with salt, so that you may know how you should respond to each person" (Colossians 4: 5, 6).

We should treasure our relationships with non-Christians. Rapport with them is a gift from God. The favor shown to Daniel by the commander of the officials came from God, and obviously it was for a purpose (Daniel 1: 9). Some of those at work, even among the unbelievers, have confidence in you. Some, who perhaps would avoid all public preaching, will listen to what you say. Along with such privilege goes much responsibility.

As in service to believers, so our ministry of good to unbelievers should have its source in the good God does for them. Does God feed and clothe the poor? Then we should expect to see members of Christ's Body engaged in this work. Is He concerned for the welfare of those under-privileged groups which society passes by: widows, orphans, the elderly, the disadvantaged, the minorities (or "strangers" in biblical language)? Then members of the Church will have ministries in these areas. Does He announce the "good news" that Christ's blood has been shed to purchase forgiveness of sin, peace with God, and eternal life? Then be sure that members of Christ's Body will be engaged in this work around the world. No one member will be able to do all the forms of work. But each of us can thank God for the many forms of ministry He has placed in the Body of Christ which contribute to the whole process of bringing in new members to complete that Body.

Andrew Murray wrote: "It is in the power of the omnipotent Saviour that the believer must find his strength for life and for work . . . . With some the chief testimony was to be that of a holy life, revealing the heaven and the Christ from whom it came. The power came to set up the Kingdom within them, to give them the victory over sin and self, to fit them by living experience to testify to the power of Jesus on the throne, to make men live in the world as saints. Others were to give themselves up entirely to the speaking in the name of Jesus. But all needed and all received the gift of power, to prove that now Jesus had received the Kingdom of the Father, all power in heaven and earth was indeed given to Him, and by Him imparted to His people just as they needed it, whether for a holy life or effective service" *(Abide in Christ)*.

7

LIGHT HOUSEKEEPING

ONCE A PERSON BEGINS TO DISCOVER how to minister to others on the job he may come to resent his ordinary chores as interruptions to his "real" work. Why should one tend a machine when he could be encouraging his fellow Christians? Why sell groceries when he could be urging non-Christians to turn from sin to Christ? But here, as in other areas of the Christian life, we must find God's balance. If our work lives are to balance, we need, in addition to the vision for on-the-job ministries, an equally clear vision of our ordinary work. God has placed us where we are to serve others, but He has also placed us there to work. What is the meaning and purpose of our ordinary work? Does it have any lasting significance?

When Daniel reported in for work each morning, he knew that ordinary earth-chores would occupy most of his time. Even after an incomparable experience from God, Daniel "carried on the king's business" (Daniel 8: 27). All Daniel's great gifts—his status of being one "greatly beloved," his place as a prophet, and an author of Scripture—did not exempt him from the daily demands of routine work. Daniel was a government official. Today we would call him a "bureaucrat." Scripture does not tell us the details of his daily work, but it probably had to do with such matters as taxation, promulgation and enforcement of regulations, planning various government projects, and attending meetings and ceremonies of state. Could such common, earth-oriented tasks please God?

We usually think of God as doing miraculous and spectacular work. He does, and always has. But God also does "ordinary" work. In the Genesis account of creation we learn of God's calling light out of darkness, separating land and water, and creating all forms of life. Spectacular, marvelous work! But once creation was complete, God undertook a very common task: He planted a garden (Genesis 2: 8). Think of it! God Himself was the world's first Farmer!

Once God had planted His garden, He delegated its care to Adam, who was "to cultivate it and keep it" (v. 15). The work of the man wasn't originally man's work at all; it was God's work. It only became man's work when God assigned it to him. Thus, even before sin entered the world, man was destined to work. The care of the earth was entrusted into man's hands. In obedience to the Creator, the man was to subdue the earth and to rule over its creatures (Genesis 1: 28). Our daily work, then, did not originate because of sin. Work is not a punishment for man's wrongdoing. It originated as a continuation, an extension, of God's activity.

God is a working God. Jesus said: "My Father is working until now, and I Myself am working" (John 5: 17). God's works are so many and so varied no man could number them. God, the Worker, created in His image man, the worker. This makes working a privilege, an honor. In working, we are doing what our heavenly Father has done since the beginning.

We men are the "housekeepers" of the earth, the resident caretakers of this planet. God is not only interested in equipping us for "spiritual" work. He also wants to train and equip us for our earthly work, whether we labor mentally or physically. To Daniel and his three friends,

"God gave them knowledge and intelligence in every branch of literature and wisdom" (Daniel 1: 17). Of Bezalel, who had charge of the construction of the Tabernacle, God said: "And I have filled him with the Spirit of God in wisdom, in understanding, in knowledge, and in all kinds of craftsmanship, to make artistic designs for work in gold, in silver, and in bronze, and in the cutting of stones for settings, and in the carving of wood, that he may work in all kinds of craftsmanship" (Exodus 31: 3–5; see also Exodus 35: 30–35). Our God is Lord of *all* the earth, of *all* our lives, not just the religious parts!

Your daily work (assuming it is a legitimate, honorable occupation) contributes something to the care of the earth. Are you a farmer? Remember that God Himself planted the first crop. Perhaps you make or sell clothing. Find a new vision for your work in Genesis 3: 21, where it is written: "And the Lord God made garments of skin for Adam and his wife, and clothed them." God started the whole business of clothing people. Your work is God's work continued. Do you prepare or serve food or beverage for others? Think back to when God fed His people manna in the wilderness. To when He commanded the ravens to bring bread and meat to a hungry Elijah. To when Jesus cooked a fish breakfast for His disciples.

If you're involved in the transportation industry, recall that God designed the first sizable ship in history, and that He opened a land bridge cross the Red Sea. Construction? God was the Architect who designed the Tabernacle. Government? The King of kings has declared that ". . . there is no authority except from God, and those which exist are established by God . . . for rulers are servants of God, devoting themselves to this very thing" (Romans 13: 1, 6). Medicine? Jesus, the Great Physician, went about "healing every kind of disease and every kind of sickness among the people" (Matthew 4: 23).

This list could be lengthened. But even these few examples make it clear that a large part of God's will for our lives centers about our daily work. For it is through our work (really His work which He assigns to us) that we carry out His first command which was to subdue the earth and rule over its creatures. The meaning of work, then, is not to be found in the work itself, but in the One who assigns the work. Only He who sends us to our work can fully answer the question: "Why work?" Meaning in our work is a gift from above. He who hears and believes God's word concerning the reason for his labor will find no task too small or insignificant.

If our work is really God's work, why is it often so frustrating? We need to remember that God's first word about work was not His last. After sin entered the world through the disobedience of Eve and Adam, God knew exactly where to touch each one's life where it would hurt the most. The woman, whose primary work was to bear children (filling the earth, Genesis 1: 28), was promised increased pain in childbirth. And the man, whose major role was to rule over and subdue the earth, was told that the earth was now his enemy. It would bring forth thorns and thistles to compete with the valuable food plants, and man would win his bread from it only by sweat and struggle. The thorn and thistle, the moth and rust, the canker and worm—all conspirators against the best efforts of man in all ages.

Why do things sometimes seem futile at work? Because "the creation was subjected to futility, not of its own will, but because of Him who subjected it . . . . For we know that the whole creation groans and suffers the pains of childbirth together until now. And not only this, but also we ourselves, having the first fruits of the Spirit, even we ourselves groan within ourselves, waiting eagerly for our adoption as sons, the redemption of our body" (Romans 8:

20, 22, 23). Even though we belong to Christ, we must still labor upon a cursed earth in bodies fashioned from the dust of that earth.

Every job has its frustrations. The farmer who pulls a weed today will discover two in its place tomorrow. The mother who mops the kitchen floor this morning will find muddy footprints there this afternoon. The retailer who did well with a particular type of merchandise last season may learn too late that the public's tastes have changed and that he is overstocked with "white elephants."

It is not unusual to see months or even years of hard work swept away by a change in the climate, the economy, or the political scene. Laboring in vain (for nothing) is a recurrent theme throughout the Scriptures. The Israelites were told from the start that if they broke their covenant with God, they would sow their seed in vain (Leviticus 26: 16, 20). Outwardly it would appear that even Daniel's daily labor was spent for nothing. Here was a man whose working hours were channeled toward building up the kingdom of Babylon. Yet the Word of God through Jeremiah was clear: "The broad wall of Babylon will be completely razed, and her high gates will be set on fire; so the peoples will toil for nothing, and the nations become exhausted only for fire" (Jeremiah 51: 58).

This being true, what a waste it would seem that Daniel's productive years were spent in building up a kingdom doomed by God for destruction. How much better it would have been, we might think, if Daniel could have devoted his efforts more toward building that Kingdom which will stand firm forever. Of how much more use Daniel might have been in "full-time Christian service"!

When we as Christians take the long look into the future, we may be tempted to feel the same about our daily work. "Only one life, 'twill soon be past, only what's done for Christ will last," we've heard since our earliest days.

We know full well that if we build a house, publish a newspaper, or sell life insurance that it will all be swept away when God discards the old earth and replaces it with the new one. If things here are so temporary, how can our daily work have any value beyond the mere earning of a living?

It is precisely at this point that we Christians may rejoice in one more benefit of our salvation. The promise of God to the Christian is this: "Therefore, my beloved brethren, be steadfast, immovable, always abounding in the work of the Lord, knowing that your toil is *not in vain in the Lord*" (1 Corinthians 15: 58). Our labor may be in vain in terms of this earth but, praise God, it is not in vain *in the Lord!*

What is the "work of the Lord"? Is it sending missionaries to foreign countries? Does it mean entering a pastorate or going into some other form of gospel work? Is the work of the Lord that which we do for our church and its program? Is it visiting, counseling, and witnessing? Yes, God's work can include all of these. But its scope is far wider, for we have just seen that the work of the Lord includes all that is necessary to keep this planet in order and to maintain life on earth.

Paul wrote that Titus should teach Christians to work to "meet pressing needs" (Titus 3:14). Life on earth involves a number of "pressing needs." And it is through the work of man that God provides many of these essentials. As we have seen previously, Scripture tells us to do our work "as for the Lord." Any work done "*for* the Lord" becomes the "work *of* the Lord."

The New Testament gives clear instructions on how slaves (employees in our day) can make certain their daily work is "in the Lord." For example, Paul wrote that slaves were to obediently carry out their masters' orders, but that in this they were to "render service, as to the Lord, and not to men, knowing that whatever good thing each one does, this he will receive back from the Lord, whether slave or free" (Ephesians 6: 7, 8). Likewise he told the Colossian slaves to "do your work heartily, as for the Lord rather than for men; knowing that from the Lord you will receive the reward of the inheritance. It is the Lord Christ whom you serve" (Colossians 3: 23, 24).

How can we keep our daily labor from being fruitless and in vain? By doing it "as to the Lord, and not to men." By serving our heavenly Employer in carrying out the orders of our earthly employers. How does this work out in practice? Suppose the boss assigns you a distasteful job. Will you follow the world's pattern? Will you waste time, put it off, think up excuses for delaying and finally turn out a half-hearted piece of work? Or will you take the boss' order as though it were an order from "the Lord Christ whom you serve," and do it carefully, promptly, and cheerfully? When the boss finds fault with the way you've handled an assignment, will you get defensive and argue the point? Slaves (employees) are not to be contradictory or argumentative (Titus 2: 9). Can you leave the justice of your cause in the hands of your heavenly Employer and submit to correction, even unjustified criticism, without hostility or bitterness? This business of dying to the self-life is not a pleasure to the flesh, but only in this way do we experience the reality of God's life-giving Spirit.

If we become "men-pleasers" in our work, our labor will ultimately prove to have been in vain. But if it is Christ whom we serve, we may also expect from Him our reward. Our heavenly Employer wants us to draw our wages from Him. The rewards which will be given in heaven are not only rewards for faithful church work and Christian service projects. God has ordered that the employee be honest on the job, do his work heartily, and respect and obey his employer—even the unreasonable employer (1 Peter 2: 18). Since these are God's orders, the Christian employee who carries them out may look forward to God's reward. Labor which brings God's reward will never be "in vain."

There is yet another sense in which our daily, earth-related work is not in vain. We have seen that God, after creating the earth, committed much of its maintenance to man. Since Christ has not yet returned, it is obvious that, for the moment at least, God wills that life continue on this present earth. For life to continue, it means that people must be fed, clothed, housed, transported, governed, and served in countless other ways. These tasks, however humble, are essential if the human race is to occupy the earth. The longing in the heart of the Christian is, "Even so, come quickly, Lord Jesus." Yet God has delayed His coming. Why? Scripture makes it clear that God has a purpose in delaying final judgment: to allow sinful man opportunity to repent and turn to Christ for salvation. "The Lord is not slow about His promise, as some count slowness, but is patient toward you, not wishing for any to perish but for all to come to repentance" (2 Peter 3: 9).

What is the implication for us who work at maintaining the earth and allowing life to continue? We are cooperating with God in His program of providing additional time for men everywhere to repent before Christ returns. By our labor we contribute to the orderly continuation of life on earth, just as we do when we pray for those in authority "that we may lead a tranquil and quiet life in all godliness and dignity. This is good and acceptable in the sight of God our Savior, who desires all men to be saved and to come to the knowledge of the truth" (1 Timothy 2: 2–4).

In a real sense we Christians are "aliens and strangers in a foreign land." Our hometown is in heaven with our Lord, and we long to be with Him. Yet for the time being, He has asked us to live "away from home," in a land under enemy occupation. Daniel and his fellow exiles were aliens and strangers in Babylon. Their hearts lay back in Jerusalem, yet God required them to live for a time in enemy territory, in Babylon.

Among the Jewish exiles some, apparently, were reluctant to put down roots. They wanted to return to Jerusalem before the full seventy years which the Lord had decreed for their exile had elapsed. To prevent this, Jeremiah the prophet wrote their elders a letter, saying: "Thus says the Lord of hosts, the God of Israel, to all the exiles whom I have sent into exile from Jerusalem to Babylon, 'Build houses and live in them; and plant gardens, and eat their produce. Take wives and become the fathers of sons and daughters, and take wives for your sons and give your daughters to husbands, that they may bear sons and daughters; and multiply there and do not decrease. And seek the welfare of the city where I have sent you into exile, and pray to the Lord on its behalf; for in its welfare you will have welfare' " (Jeremiah 29: 4–7).

God wants His people to be very much involved in the basic functions necessary to maintaining life on this earth. Though this world is not our final home, we are to settle down to work in it and for it while we are here. Of course this does not mean we are to set our hearts on it. We must continue looking and longing for the new Jerusalem. Our engagement in the tasks of this world, though extremely important, is temporary. Jesus indicated that His people would continue to work in ordinary occupations right up to the moment of His return. He told His disciples how it will be when the Son of Man comes: "Then there shall be two men in the field; one will be taken, and one will be left. Two women will be grinding at the mill; one will be taken, and one will be left" (Matthew 24: 40, 41). Farm work and food preparation— two examples of the many jobs which will be occupying God's people when Christ returns. What an encouragement! Of all the examples He could have used, Jesus chose this picture of people in ordinary work being caught up from their earthly tasks to meet Him at His return!

In that day, all will be changed. No longer will we battle a cursed earth. No more frustrating labor. "For behold, I create new heavens and a new earth; and the former things shall not be remembered or come to mind . . . . For as the lifetime of a tree, so shall be the days of My people, and My chosen ones shall wear out [long enjoy] the work of their hands. They shall not labor in vain . . . ." (Isaiah 65: 17, 22, 23).

What a day that is going to be! Praise God!

8

SECRETS OF A LIGHT HEAVYWEIGHT

As a small boy growing up on a farm I usually had several projects under way. In my own way I kept very busy, yet my business had very little relationship to the business of the farm. But as years passed, Dad began to expect some profitable work from me. By my teen years I had become an "old hand" around the place.

What brought about the change? How could a small boy, bent only on his own private projects, be transformed into a teenager who contributed significantly to the success of the farm? As I look back, one factor stands out: I learned to work by watching my father work. On the tractor, around the barn, and in the repair shop, I learned to work properly by watching how Dad did it.

The same principle holds true in our Christian lives. Our work is rooted in God's work. If we would learn how to do our daily work "as to the Lord," we must watch God at work. Through the new birth we have become sons of God—his life is in us. But no son is made complete by birth alone. Maturity comes through spending time with the Father and through watching Him work.

On the farm my "work" in those early years originated in my own imagination. In that sense it was my own work. But as I grew older, Dad's work became my work. I only continued what he had done for years. Our work as Christians should be nothing more than God's work continued. In fact, apart from sin, man's work has nothing original about it. It might even be said that our work on earth is simply a copy of God's work. When we see our work in this light, as a copy of the heavenly Original, we touch one of the deepest truths Scripture would teach us. From Genesis to Revelation the theme is there: the true Original in heaven should be the pattern for all that takes place on earth.

As in heaven, so on earth—this should be the guiding principle behind our everyday work. Our first need, then, is a clear vision of the heavenly pattern. Only by seeing God at work can we pattern our work accordingly. Do we really know how God works? Faulty vision can defeat us. We may have only foggy notions of how God works. Much of what we know of God may have come only by hearsay from second- or thirdhand sources. As Job had to admit after saying many mouthfuls of words about God: "I have heard of Thee by the hearing of the ear; but now my eye sees Thee" (Job 42: 5).

Knowing God by report has its value, but only as a starting point, as a stimulus to search Him out and find Him for ourselves. The "forty-niners" of the gold rush days were not content with merely hearing of gold in California. The report spurred them into a wholehearted search, until they actually held the gold in their own hands. If we depend too long upon knowing God only by report, we will soon become disillusioned by conflicting reports. Like Job, we need a personal vision of God through our own eye of faith. Without such vision we can never really be certain of how God works, and will have little on which to pattern our own work.

How can we enter into a vision of how God works? Certainly not through any single mountaintop experience. Peter was able to recognize Jesus as "the Christ, the

Son of the living God," because of a revelation from heaven (Matthew 16:16). Yet this one revelation was not enough to teach him how God works. Only moments later Jesus had to tell Peter: ". . . you are not setting your mind on God's interests, but man's" (v. 23). One seeing was not enough. Peter needed more.

And so do we. One look will not suffice. A. W. Tozer once described faith as "the gaze of a soul upon a saving God" *(The Pursuit of God)*. To gaze suggests more than a brief glance. It suggests long and careful looking, with the attention of the whole person focused upon its object. If we would see how God works, so that we may pattern our daily work accordingly, it will require a lifelong gaze upon Him.

This means spending our lives in a place where God is "visible" to the eye of faith. On the farm, I could observe my father going about his work because I lived with him. Had I spent only summers or occasional weekends with him, I would have missed seeing a large part of his work. How could I fully have understood harvest if I had missed seeing plowing, planting, cultivating, and irrigating? The same holds true of our spiritual gaze. The fullness of God's work will not appear to one who simply visits Him now and again. Such vision is reserved for those who live in His presence. This is why Jesus commands us: "Abide [live] in Me." Only by living in Jesus, and therefore in the Father, are we in a position to observe all of God's works. "Great are the works of the Lord; they are studied by all who delight in them. Splendid and majestic is His work. . ." (Psalm 111: 2, 3).

Is this too much to expect? Is it possible for one who works in Babylon to abide in Christ, to gaze continually upon God, to study and delight in His works? There appear to be too many distractions. All the urgent voices and responsibilities of this world crowd in upon us, and we seem unable to abide in Him who speaks in the still small voice. If our work centered more in spiritual concerns, we imagine, it would be easier to abide consistently in Christ. We may even envy those in gospel work, thinking that such occupations would permit more opportunity for the soul to gaze upon God.

If we think that abiding in Christ is a work completely dependent upon us to perform, it *will* prove impossible in everyday work. We can no more keep ourselves in Christ by our own effort than we can provide our own salvation initially. But God did not just forgive our sins and leave the rest up to us. No, He has "blessed us with *every* spiritual blessing in the heavenly places in Christ. . ." (Ephesians 1: 3). One of these spiritual blessings is a place to live, to abide, in Christ. Scripture makes it plain that God has seated us "in the heavenly places, in Christ Jesus" Ephesians 2: 6). God has already placed us in Christ. He has provided each Christian a place to sit in Christ. Our part is simply to accept the fact, rest in His promise, and stay seated there! "He who dwells in the shelter of the Most High will abide in the shadow of the Almighty" (Psalm 91: 1).

To remain in our earthly bodies requires no thought or effort on our part. We continue to inhabit our bodies even while asleep. So it is with our spiritual life in Christ. Our place in Him remains intact even when our thoughts and activities must be wholly occupied with earthly chores. We can count on His keeping us there all the time, no matter where our jobs may carry us on this earth. The temptation we face is this: to think of the abiding life only in terms of specifically religious activity. It's easy to believe that we are abiding in Christ while in a church service, reading the Bible, or at prayer. But on the job, since we cannot keep our attention on Him, we no longer feel His nearness. Or if we think God has little interest in ordinary work, we may feel that He leaves us at the shop or office door.

If faced with this test, we need to remember two things. First, even our daily tasks are God's work. He is fully as concerned with them as with our more apparently religious activities. And secondly, the work of abiding is a work of faith—believing that God is keeping us in Christ every moment. This is not a work of our own mental effort. God will keep us in Christ, in the secret "sitting room." We simply rely on Him to hold us there, on the job, anywhere.

By faith in God's promised provision, then, we may count on abiding in Christ without interruption all through each day. But as long as we occupy these earthly bodies we will also need to set aside special times to come alone into the presence of God. Our physical senses, assaulted by all the voices and pressures of life, must often retreat into the secret living room where heaven's realities may occupy our total attention, where God's work may become "visible" as a pattern for our work. Jesus said, "When you pray, go into your inner room, and when you have shut your door, pray to your Father who is in secret . . ." (Matthew 6: 6). The Christian who works in Babylon cannot do without these times in the secret place. Not that these times are more holy than our hours at work. It is only that our work hours demand attention to temporal duties. In our times of retreat we are freed to be wholly attentive to what God speaks to us. These times in the secret place are the "staff meetings" between the heavenly Employer and the one who serves Him. The whole of each work day belongs to Him, but the special meetings are needed so that the work may be properly directed.

Daniel would rank in the "heavyweight" class among God's lights in the world. He knew the value of these hidden staff meetings with God. We who work in the world can profit by studying the agendas of the meetings which took place between this man and his heavenly Employer. Our outward service on the job will be no stronger than our inward relationship with Him whom we serve. The key to Daniel's success as a government worker in Babylon lay not in his great ability, but in his faithfulness in meeting God in the secret place. What Daniel saw there sustained him in every area of his work life.

Daniel's "inner room" was apparently a roof chamber in his own house. Three times each day he entered this place to meet God. Though Daniel's work schedule is unknown to us, the timing of his meetings with God seems very much up to date and adaptable for most of us who work today. The first meeting marks the very beginning of the work day—a time for committing the entire day into the Lord's hands and seeking His guidance in any decisions that must be made. The second meeting fits well into a lunch break. It offers a chance for a midday examination of our walk, for confessions and correction if needed, and for renewed commitment. Most of us can find an "inner room" at work. Somewhere there is a place to get alone with God, even if this means taking a walk to be alone.

The third meeting quite naturally falls at the end of the day. Here we place before God the whole day for His review. There may be lessons to be learned, confessions of failure, praise for victories, or new promises for the following day.

Three meetings a day may not always be possible because of schedule conflicts and other interruptions. But who ever said staff meetings had to be held on a rigid schedule? Sometimes regular meetings must be canceled. Other times unique situations and needs all require special "nonscheduled" meetings. The whole point is to carry out the instructions of our heavenly Employer, not to set some sort of perfect attendance record for staff meetings. While Daniel's custom of meeting God three times a day seems ideally suited to the typical modern workday, we should never make such a schedule a legalistic rule.

The Scriptures offer us glimpses into some of the things that occurred during Daniel's meetings with God. We have our first view of Daniel alone with his God immediately after Nebuchadnezzar's dream had been revealed to him in a vision at night. As we peer into that secret meeting place, we see Daniel worshiping and praising God. His words of gratitude and praise read like a psalm (Daniel 2: 20–23).

On the surface, worship and our daily work may appear to be as far apart as heaven and earth. Yet they are closely linked. As Daniel worshiped God he observed His rulership over times and seasons and earthly authorities. He recognized that wisdom and power originate with God, and come only as gifts to men. He saw God as the revealer of truth. As Daniel worshiped, he saw something of how God works. In worship he observed the ways of God.

Only as we make a habit of gazing in adoration at the heavenly Original can we pattern our works after His works. The close link between worship and work was expressed beautifully by David: "Let Thy work appear to Thy servants . . . . And do confirm for us the work of our hands; yes, confirm the work of our hands" (Psalm 90: 16, 17).

A vision of the heavenly Original will begin developing in the man who worships God daily. He will begin to see the pattern in its purity and beauty. Such vision is not always comfortable to live with. Inner turmoil, groaning, and longing will grip the heart of the one who sees not only earth's Babylon but heaven's Holy City as well. Why? Because everywhere he looks on earth the divine pattern has been ignored, broken by man-made tradition, or plainly rejected. Jesus knew this longing. His eyes had seen the heavenly Jerusalem, but He also saw the earthly city by that name. You can hear His anguish as He cries: "O Jerusalem, Jerusalem, the city that kills the prophets and stones those sent to her! How often I wanted to gather your children together, just as a hen gathers her brood under her wings, and you would not have it!" (Luke 13: 34).

As the pressure of this longing mounts it must find a release. Prayer is that release. Though powerless in ourselves to bring about the needed reform in a single life or an entire planet, we can call out for help to the One who has that power. The more clearly we see the contrast between what is true in heaven and what takes place on earth, the more we will pray. No one has seen this contrast more clearly than Jesus. Originally from above, He emptied Himself to live for a time on our soil. Jesus has seen it from both sides. And what occupies Him now that He has ascended to the Father's right hand? He prays. No wonder one of the most frequent commands in the New Testament is that Christians give themselves to prayer. Prayer work is being done in heaven by Jesus. Therefore, it ought to be done by His servants on earth. What is true there should also be true here.

The God who created the universe by means of His word, who now sustains it all by His word, also rules it by His word. And He has given us, His sons, the privilege of coming to Him in Christ requesting that this or that word of command be issued. What higher privilege could any created being want? Have you seen something of the heavenly pattern? Do you long to see it followed on earth? Go to God in prayer and ask that a word of command be issued that what you have seen in heaven may be true on earth. Have you had a difficulty knowing the will of God in prayer? Ask Him to show you more of the heavenly pattern. As we see more of that pattern, the better able we are to pray. Why? Because we know that His will is done in heaven, and that He desires it to be done on earth as well. Thank God we may ask in confidence. For once the word has been issued, nothing can prevent the command from being carried out.

There are no limits to the range of our requests. It may be that we will be asking for new strength or vision in our own lives. Or we may pray on behalf of our neighbors on the job—Christians and non-Christians. Perhaps our work itself has brought along difficulties and challenges. Yes, we may ask God to deliver us even here, remembering that all our work is His work. We, as citizens of God's Kingdom, are to allow His rule to extend into every area of our lives.

Asking is only one part of prayer. Admitting is another. We must admit before God where we have gone wrong, where we have failed to follow the heavenly pattern. Daniel, after seeing the pattern through reading the Scriptures, was driven to his knees in a prayer of confession (Daniel 9: 4–19). It is significant to notice whose sins Daniel confessed. Today much emphasis is given to our need as individuals to confess our own sins. This is right as far as it goes. But Daniel went further. He confessed sins in four areas. He confessed his own personal sin and the sins of the whole body of God's people (v. 20), and the sins of Israel's leaders and the sins of Israel's forefathers (v. 8).

There is such a thing as individual guilt, and this must be confessed. But there is also such a thing as corporate guilt, and we are to confess this as readily as individual wrongdoing. The whole company of God's people or any of its leaders may stray. This is why God provided a special blood sacrifice for corporate sin and for sins of the leaders of His people (Leviticus 4: 13–26). And this is why the call to repentance which is sounded in the second and third chapters of Revelation is a call for whole churches to repent, not for individual repentance. Corporate sin is

frequently brought about by following man-made traditions rather than what God has spoken. For this reason,
confession of the sins of our ancestors (whether physical
or spiritual ancestors) is extremely important. Daniel worshiped the God of his fathers (Daniel 2: 23), but he also
acknowledged the sin of his fathers. Unless we, too, recognize and confess the sins of our spiritual forefathers, we
will be bound by their human traditions. And if we are
bound by their traditions, the Word of God will to that
extent be rendered powerless in our lives (Matthew 15: 6).

If we want our work to line up with God's work, confession is vital. We may long to follow the heavenly pattern in
our work on earth, but to do so will mean a readiness to
admit failure. Without confession, how will we hear God
speak the word of forgiveness which is ours through
Christ's blood? How will we be ready to receive His word
of correction and adjustment? Failure to follow the pattern can be forgiven. But what remedy is there for failure
to recognize and admit the failure? Even in our work lives
the enemy roams about searching for accusations to hurl
against us before the throne of God. Satan will readily
confess our sins there. Our only defense lies in honestly
admitting any error before God so that the blood of Jesus
can cancel all condemnation, shutting the mouth of the
enemy.

There is more to observe in Daniel's secret place. He
practiced fasting (Daniel 9: 3; 10: 2, 3). Fasting is inti-
mately related to prayer, and is often used in waging
spiritual warfare which requires strenuous measures. In
chapter 10, Daniel undertook a three-week fast in order to
seek out a difficult message from God. At the end of the
three weeks, a messenger appeared to him who assured
Daniel that "from the first day that you set your heart on
understanding this and on humbling yourself before your
God, your words were heard . . ." (v. 12). We usually

think of Daniel as a man of great humility, yet even he needed to humble himself. Fasting can be an aid here. In Psalm 35: 13, David wrote: "I humbled, my soul with fasting."

Working in the world may have its humbling moments. But it also provides many stimulants to pride. A job well done may bring compliments and much admiration from co-workers. Babylon is filled with fertilizer for the pride of life, and we Christians are not immune to the growth of that weed. Yet we dare not let it grow, for we know that "God is opposed to the proud, but gives grace to the humble" (James 4: 6). Going without food, in itself, will not automatically make us humble. But if the Spirit of God leads us to fast, He is able to use this means in humbling us before Him.

In Daniel 9: 2 we see Daniel reading Scripture, a passage from Jeremiah. Daniel was not only a man of worship, prayer, confession, and fasting, but also a man who knew the written Word of God. This is yet another essential in the life of one who would have his daily work count for God. As Paul assured Timothy: "All Scripture is inspired by God and profitable for teaching, for reproof, for correction, for training in righteousness; that the man of God may be adequate, *equipped for every good work*" (2 Timothy 3: 16, 17). How is it that that the Scriptures equip us for work?

Jesus made it plain in His parables that God's Word is like seed. What is a seed? A seed is a capsule which carries a specific kind of life. Seeds carried by the wind from one living plant can drop into soil a great distance away and produce many other living plants like the parent plant. Spiritual life from God comes to us in the same way. God's words are like capsules, carrying spiritual life from their source (Jesus) to us. These word-capsules must be carried into our hearts by God's Holy Spirit. What are the practical implications? If I want to have an abundance of God's harvest in my work, I must allow Him to plant an abundance of His seed, the Word of God, in my heart. For "whatever a man sows, this he will also reap" (Galatians 6: 7).

So our times in the secret place should also be times for planting, for hiding the Word of God deeply away. If we do, we can be certain that one day our lives will begin to produce works originating from heaven instead of earth. As David put it: "Thy word I have treasured in my heart, that I may not sin against Thee" (Psalm 119: 11). Only in this way will we find sufficient life within to withstand the forces in Babylon as they pull toward the world's pattern and toward death. "I have written to you, young men, because you are strong, and the word of God abides in you, and you have overcome the evil one" (1 John 2: 14).

Many "pests" are loose in the world which would eat away at the life begun by the seed of God's Word. Jesus warned that "the worries of the world, and the deceitfulness of riches, and the desires for other things enter in and choke the word, and it becomes unfruitful" (Mark 4: 19). Christianity is not so much a matter of learning doctrines as it is a matter of life. Life can be increased, or life can be "choked." Thus, I do not read the Scriptures merely to learn good doctrines, but I read and retain to draw fresh supplies of life from the Source. The seed of God's Word, carried into my heart by His Holy Spirit, brings me new life from heaven.

A close look into Daniel's life reveals another secret about how he spent his times apart with God. At the end of chapter seven, following a magnificent revelation from heaven concerning Christ and God's Kingdom, Daniel admits, "my thoughts were greatly alarming me and my face grew pale, but I kept the matter to myself" (or literally, "in my heart"). Daniel worshiped, prayed, confessed, fasted, studied the Scriptures—and also meditated upon the truths God revealed to him. He was not one who received the words of God lightly, nor did he forget them quickly. Once the seed of God's Word had lodged in Daniel's heart, he kept it there and allowed it time to spring into productive life. He was one of those men of God described in the first Psalm whose "delight is in the law of the Lord, and in His law he meditates day and night" (Psalm 1: 2).

The word "recollection" used to convey the same meaning as meditation. It is unfortunate that the word has lost that meaning for us today. For actually in meditation we are able to "re-collect," to collect together again, the words God has spoken deep in our innermost heart. We who work in crowded, noisy offices, supermarkets, or shops know that the pressures of life among people tend to bombard us and scatter the precious seed of God's Word. For this reason, we desperately need times of meditation and quietness where, with God's help, we may recollect the bits and pieces, the rebukes and promises, the commands and comforts of His words to us.

In spite of our fast-paced age, the Christian who works must find time for meditation, reflection, recollection. For in meditation, as in worship, prayer, and Bible study, we may mull over the works and words of God. David pondered the works of God. He wrote: "I remember the days of old; I meditate on all Thy doings; I muse on the work of Thy hands" (Psalm 143: 5). And again, "I will meditate on all Thy work, and muse on Thy deeds" (Psalm 77: 12). How vital that we see the pattern! Otherwise, how can our work on earth be of any value?

A habit of meditation will not come easily. Every attraction in the world is aimed against it. If we would meditate we must be totally convinced of its value in ordering our work after God's work. And then, seeing its worth, we must "die" to the pull of many activities to which the world or even a church program may call us, so that we may devote significant periods of time to turning our attention wholly to the Word within us. Then we will know the joy of obeying the command: "Let the word of Christ richly dwell within you . . ." (Colossians 3: 16).

These brief glimpses into Daniel's "staff meetings" with his heavenly Employer tell us why his light so brightened Babylon. Daniel bore fruit for God on the job only because He knew how to abide as a branch in the Vine. His good works did not come through working harder, but through a more complete union with the Source of heaven's life. In previous chapters we considered several ministries of light with which we ought to be serving Christians and non-Christians as we work in our ordinary jobs. Perhaps you agree that these ministries are needed, yet feel overwhelmed by your own weakness and lack of fruit in these areas. How can your on-the-job ministries be increased?

Christians have often been chided for their lack of concern for non-Christians and have been urged to "Get busy and witness harder on the job." Or they sometimes hear that the key to a more fruitful life is to "Get more involved in Christian service activities." Hanging apples on the branches of a non-producing tree may improve its appearance temporarily, but this is not fruit-bearing. If an orchardist wants a low-production apple tree to yield more apples, he nurtures the life of the tree. He knows that he cannot directly increase fruit-bearing; he can only work through the life that is in the tree.

This truth is borne out by one of Jesus' parables: "A certain man had a fig tree which had been planted in his vineyard; and he came looking for fruit on it, and did not find any. And he said to the vineyard-keeper, 'Behold, for three years I have come looking for fruit on this fig tree without finding any. Cut it down! Why does it even use up the ground?' And he answered and said to him, 'Let it alone, sir, for this year too, until I dig around it and put in fertilizer; and if it bears fruit next year, fine; but if not, cut it down' " (Luke 13: 6–9).

It does no good to pressure ourselves or other Christians to produce an immediate display of fruit. Too often, such urgings only result in more self-effort. Any increase in our on-the-job ministries must spring from an increase of Christ's life within us. A heavy crop of fruit requires a strong system of roots. First the roots, then the fruits. As our roots become more firmly established in Christ, the fruits will follow spontaneously. As Jesus put it, "He who abides in Me, and I in him, he bears much fruit; for apart from Me you can do nothing" (John 15: 5). Real fruit results only from abiding in Christ.

Have you wished God could use you more in ministering to other Christians near you on the job? Are you wondering how your witness to non-Christians at work can be strengthened? Let Daniel's example guide you. Focus the gaze of your soul on Jesus. Learn how to abide in Him. Fix your eyes on our Savior, "the author and perfecter of faith . . ." (Hebrews 12: 2). As His life increases within you, so will His light.

9

THE ADDED THINGS

WHILE WE WORK AND BEAR FRUIT in this world, our roots are to be in heaven. Yet the world has its own root system. With a constant pull, like gravity, Babylon summons its inhabitants to strike their roots downward into its soil. Scripture tells us that "the love of money is a root of all sorts of evil . . ." (1 Timothy 6: 10). Money, perhaps more than any other single earthly thing, can lead to entanglement in the world's root system. As Christians who work in ordinary jobs, we must continually handle money. Here, then, is a test. What does money mean to us? The practical answers to this question will tell us much about where our roots are planted.

What about Daniel? Did his daily meetings with God enable him to pass the "root test"? How well did he escape the money snare? Was his attitude toward the dollar any different from that of the typical worldling? Between the fourth and fifth chapters of the Book of Daniel great changes took place. Nebuchadnezzar was no longer king. In his place his grandson Belshazzar now ruled. Typically, when the power at the top shifted, the subordinate ranks felt the effects. Daniel, who had been "ruler over the whole province of Babylon and chief prefect over all the wise men of Babylon" during Nebuchadnezzar's reign, was now a nobody. King Belshazzar did not even know him.

But one day the new king met a problem beyond his powers. During one of his extravagant gorging and drinking parties, he and his guests were greatly shaken when a hand appeared and wrote some strange words on the plastered wall. An event like this couldn't be ignored, but who could translate the writing? Though his knees were knocking with fright, the king did not forget how to stir up his staff's enthusiasm for extra effort. "Any man who can read this inscription and explain its interpretation to me will be clothed with purple, and have a necklace of gold around his neck, and have authority as third ruler in the kingdom," he promised (Daniel 5: 7). But the usual bait, gold and glory, failed to work this time. No one could read the handwriting on the wall.

Just as what little color was left drained from the king's face, the queen entered the banquet hall and told the king to cheer up: she had the solution. There was, she said, a man named Daniel in the kingdom who had solved problems like this one during the reign of Nebuchadnezzar. So Daniel was summoned and brought before the king. Belshazzar outlined the problem to Daniel, and repeated his promise of promotion if Daniel could tell him what the writing meant.

Had Daniel been a typical Babylonian bureaucrat, his thoughts might have gone something like this: "It's about time someone in this new administration recognized my talent and experience. I've spent long enough at this underpaid, obscure job. Now's my chance to make a comeback."

But Daniel's answer was far different. He said, "Keep your gifts for yourself, or give your rewards to someone else; however, I will read the inscription to the king and make the interpretation known to him" (Daniel 5: 17). His answer makes it clear: you can't "buy" a man whose roots are in heaven. Money and position are not the motivating drives which keep him going. Verse twenty-nine indicates that Belshazzar went ahead and gave Daniel all the things he had promised anyway. But this is beside the point. The real point is Daniel's detachment from the "main things" this world has to offer. Since his heart was not attached to the world, not rooted in the Babylon system, he could take or leave the things its inhabitants counted of value. Either way, having things or not having them, his roots were undisturbed. Yes, Daniel passed the "root test."

This incident from Daniel's life is a perfect example of what Jesus meant when He told His followers: "Do not be anxious then, saying, 'What shall we eat?' or, 'What shall we drink?' or, 'With what shall we clothe ourselves?' For all these things the Gentiles eagerly seek; for your heavenly Father knows that you need all these things. But seek first His kingdom, and His righteousness; and *all these things shall be added* to you" (Matthew 6: 31–33). Daniel, in making his first concern the kingdom of God, found that God abundantly provided for all his needs in the kingdom of Babylon. And through it all, Daniel's heart was at rest, free from anxiety, because he was not directly seeking anything from the world. He was freed from the unrest of political maneuvering, back-stabbing, and self-promotion that a typical man of the world would employ to obtain such a high position.

It is easy for the Christian to get caught up in the world's struggle to pad the paycheck. But we should be careful not to follow the world's lead and begin itching after more money for the world's reasons, or attempt to get it through the world's methods. The world's way is to go after things directly. If an employee wants higher pay, he attempts to persuade the boss he needs a raise. When the individual attempt fails, he joins with other employees to gain "leverage," or "clout," or "muscle." This begins a chain reaction of bargaining and a never-ending hassle between two sides. But is this the way marked out by God?

James asks: "But what about the feuds and struggles that exist among you—where do you suppose they come from? Can't you see that they arise from conflicting passions within yourselves? You crave for something and don't get it; you are murderously jealous of what others have got and which you can't possess yourselves; you struggle and fight with one another. You don't get what you want because you don't ask God for it. And when you do ask He doesn't give it to you, for you ask in quite the wrong spirit—you want only to satisfy your own desires" (James 4: 1–3, *Phillips*).

There can be no doubt that wages are important and highly desirable to working people. Does Scripture offer the Christian employee any guidelines in this area? Is God really concerned about such things as raises and promotions? Or does He care to get this closely involved in ordinary work?

Before attempting to find answers to these questions, perhaps we should first ask the question: Would a really spiritual person even work for wages? This may seem at first to be hardly worth asking. Most of us could name several persons whom we consider to be walking closely with God and who work for wages. But the question needs to be raised and settled in our own hearts and minds, not for those others who work for wages, but for ourselves individually. For there seems to have sprung up a notion that God would be more pleased if we all were to "live by faith" (meaning without any regular income) than to draw an hourly wage or monthly salary.

Our search for the answer to this question could begin in the Book of Leviticus. God instructed the Israelites: "The wages of a hired man are not to remain with you all night until morning" (19: 13). We are given added insight into this command in Deuteronomy 24: 15: "You shall give him his wages on his day before the sun sets, for he is poor and sets his heart on it; so that he may not cry against you to the Lord and it become sin in you." How could wage-earning possibly be unacceptable when God counts non-payment of wages due as sin?

John the Baptist, so far as we know, did not work for wages. But when he answered some soldiers about their responsibility before God, he did not tell them to renounce their status as wage-earners. Instead, he told them, "be content with your wages" (Luke 3: 14). Paul, the apostle, wrote that an ex-thief was to get a job and earn enough so that he could stop taking and start giving (Ephesians 4: 28). As we saw previously, Paul was so convinced of the rightness of wage-earning that he worked at a trade himself to set an example to be followed by the Thessalonians (2 Thessalonians 3: 8, 9).

God has called *all* saints to live by faith. Some of them "get their living from the gospel" (1 Corinthians 9: 14). Others get their living from wages, commissions, or profits. It is not a question of better or worse, but one of obedience. What has God summoned me to do? Am I willing to receive my daily bread by whatever avenue God chooses to provide it? Would I be willing to live by the gospel if He asked me to do that? Or to work for wages if that were His call?

Once we are confident that God calls many to be wage-earners, another question suggests itself: What about raises in pay? The world certainly knows how to go after pay boosts. But how does the Christian cope with a shortage of funds? After all, inflation touches him too!

Earlier we saw that Scripture instructs us to do our work "as to the Lord, and not to men." This should give us our first clue: the Christian is answerable first to his heavenly Employer. The man of the world can go no higher than his earthly employer. But the Christian may appeal to God for help. Has God approved any motives for wanting more money? The Bible marks out at least four legitimate reasons for desiring money (not loving money, but wanting it for proper uses).

The first area concerns our own needs. Paul wrote that the Thessalonian believers were to "make it your ambition to lead a quiet life and attend to your own business and work with your hands, just as we commanded you; so that you may behave properly toward outsiders and not be in any need" (1 Thessalonians 4: 11, 12). He repeated his instructions in his second letter to this same church: "If anyone will not work, neither let him eat. For we hear that some among you are leading an undisciplined life, doing no work at all, but acting like busybodies. Now such persons we command and exhort in the Lord Jesus Christ to work in quiet fashion and eat their own bread" (2 Thessalonians 3: 10–12).

We are also instructed to work so that we may provide for the needs of members of our families. Paul assured Timothy that "if any one does not provide for his own, and especially for those of his household, he has denied the faith, and is worse than an unbeliever" (1 Timothy 5: 8). The needs of parents and grandparents are a part of our responsibility, for we are told that "if any widow has children or grandchildren, let them first learn to practice piety in regard to their own family, and to make some return to their parents; for this is acceptable in the sight of God" (1 Timothy 5: 4). The command to honor father and mother includes honoring them with our material wealth, for it was this command that Jesus cited when He faulted the scribes and Pharisees for teaching a devious way to avoid giving to parents (Mark 7: 10–12). We may conclude, then, that any shortages of funds to meet our own needs, the needs of our families, or others in our sphere of responsibility can be legitimate motivation for asking God to increase our pay.

Secondly, Scripture tells us to give of our material goods to those who instruct us in the faith. "And let the one who is taught the word share all good things with him who teaches" (Galatians 6: 6). Many who preach or teach may forego this right, as Paul sometimes did. But it is clearly scriptural that a worker in God's Garden, the Church, should enjoy some of the material produce. The desire to give more to those who teach us in the faith is a second legitimate reason for asking our heavenly Employer for additional funds.

Closely related to this second area is a third: that of helping to support Christian workers who have gone out to reach others. John praised a fellow believer, Gaius, for practicing this sort of giving: "Beloved, you are acting faithfully in whatever you accomplish for the brethren, and especially when they are strangers; and they bear witness to your love before the church; and you will do well to send them on their way in a manner worthy of God. For they went out for the sake of the Name, accepting nothing from the Gentiles. Therefore we ought to support such men, that we may be fellow-workers with the truth" (3 John 5–8). Here is what we commonly call "missionary giving," springing from the God-given right of those who proclaim the gospel to earn their living from the gospel (1 Corinthians 9: 14).

In the Great Commission, Jesus told His Church to go into every part of the world proclaiming the gospel. Obviously, He did not mean for every single individual to go into every part of the world. An apostle, one who is sent, a missionary, goes. An elder, as one of the shepherds in a local church, stays—as do those allotted to his care. But without the support of those who stay and work to earn and give, how could the others go? Thus, by our joint participation, each doing the part assigned by God, we corporately carry out Jesus' command to go. If our desire for more money stems from our wanting to engage more heavily in missionary giving, then we stand on scriptural ground in making our request.

There is yet another use for our funds described in Scripture: that of giving to the poor and needy. The Bible has more to say about our responsibilities for giving here than in any other area. Many Old Testament passages remind God's people to remember the poor. For example: "Is this not the fast which I choose . . . ? Is it not to divide your bread with the hungry, and bring the homeless poor into the house; when you see the naked, to cover him; and not to hide yourself from your own flesh [i.e., not to disappear when your own relatives are in need]?" (Isaiah 58: 6, 7). Daniel, in advising Nebuchadnezzar how to break away from his sins, told him to show mercy to the poor (Daniel 4: 27).

The major emphasis upon giving in the New Testament is upon sharing with other Christians who are in need—in keeping with the priority in the command to do good to all men, *especially* to those who are of the household of the faith. "But whoever has the world's goods, and beholds his brother in need and closes his heart against him, how does the love of God abide in him?" (1 John 3: 17). But the "all men" must also include the neighbor, whom we are to love as we love ourselves. In this work, as in all our work, we are to follow the pattern of the heavenly Original, who causes His rain to fall upon both the just and the unjust.

Jesus often urged those who would follow Him to sell their possessions and give to the poor. And He must have practiced what He preached, for when Judas left the last supper with the common money box, the other disciples thought that perhaps Jesus had privately instructed him to go out and give something to the poor (John 13: 29). Jesus foretold the sobering words that will be spoken in judgment over this matter of giving. Our care for the poor (or lack of it) shows our care for Christ. To feed and clothe them is to feed and clothe Him (Matthew 25: 41–45).

We can be confident, then, that if we are asking God for more pay in order to meet needs in any of these four areas (i.e., providing for our own family needs, sharing with those who teach or preach, supporting missionary work, and giving to those in need), we are asking for help in areas approved by Him.

But we should also bear in mind the pitfalls which surround the dollar, and search our hearts honestly to see whether there may not be something else in our motivation for more money. For more money, gone after for the wrong reason, can ruin us. Paul warned Timothy that "those who want to get rich fall into temptation and a snare and many foolish and harmful desires which plunge men into ruin and destruction" (1 Timothy 6: 9). To get rich usually means that a man must hoard his wealth, and hoarding is contrary to God's way of working. God "gives to all men generously" (James 1: 5), and consequently He loves a cheerful giver.

While riches have always been a snare to God's people, the snare today is even more subtle in our affluent societies. It is easy not to think of ourselves as "rich," since we can point to so many who have far more money than ourselves. Yet an outstanding characteristic of the rich man is his ability to live in comfort and pleasure. Scripture tells us that in the last days men will be "lovers of pleasure rather than lovers of God" (2 Timothy 3: 4). We would do well to let Jesus' words search us often: "But woe to you who are rich, for you are receiving your comfort in full. Woe to you who are well-fed now, for you shall be hungry. Woe to you who laugh now, for you shall mourn and weep" (Luke 6: 24, 25).

Assuming our motives are the right ones, how do we approach our heavenly Employer in asking for more money? We know that an earthly employer would examine our past performance in considering a request for a raise. Is there anything we can do to assure that our request for added pay will get a favorable hearing? Jesus left us with some invaluable advice here: "Give, and it will be given to you; good measure, pressed down, shaken together, running over, they will pour into your lap. For whatever measure you deal out to others, it will be dealt to you in return" (Luke 6: 38). How have we given from what we already have? That is the criterion by which our heavenly Employer will judge our request for more. If our habit has been one of giving, our request will be honored in heaven.

Many Christians have claimed the scriptural promise in Philippians 4: 19: "And my God shall supply all your needs according to His riches in glory in Christ Jesus." It is important that we notice the context in which this promise was originally given. The Philippian believers had shared their wealth with Paul to help supply his needs. Paul called their gift "a fragrant aroma, an acceptable sacrifice, well pleasing to God." After they had given of their money to another Christian, it was then that the promise came from heaven that their own needs would be met. In claiming this Philippian promise of supply, we should not forget to follow the Philippian practice of sharing.

Most of what has been said on raises can be applied to promotions as well. Christians who work in the world often wonder: Is it right to be ambitious, to want to rise to the top in my organization? Again, we should search our motives. God has commanded us to put our whole heart into whatever we do, and this includes our work. Men who approach their work wholeheartedly are often honored by promotion. Daniel was promoted several times, but there is no indication in Scripture that he directly sought promotion. He humbled himself, made himself low before God, and God saw to his promotions. Yet Daniel was able also to take *de*motion without complaining and without lusting for the top spot. Like Paul, he knew both "how to get along with humble means" and "how to live in prosperity" (Philippians 4: 12). Why? Because Daniel had his heart set on the kingdom of God before everything else. His ups and downs in terms of this earth didn't matter, for he knew his final destination was secure. God gave him the assurance that "you will enter into rest and rise again for your allotted portion at the end of the age" (Daniel 12: 13).

Like Daniel, we who follow Christ should keep our priorities in the proper order. Our central attention should be focused upon Christ, not upon the "main things" of this world. For us the "main thing" is the kingdom of God and His righteousness, to allow our righteous King to rule us on this earth. Anything else is not the "main thing," but simply an "added thing.' Our added things can bring enjoyment, but must be held with palm up and open. While we should not become unduly attached to them, we ought to thank God for these added things, for they come as reminders that God is not only our heavenly Employer, but our generous and loving Father as well.

10

THE REST AREAS

IF PAYDAY RATES AS THE FAVORITE DAY among people who work, Friday ranks a close second. Payday brings the reward for working. Friday brings the rest from working. Late Friday afternoon, for many people, is welcomed as a chance to escape the burdens of the week. As the gateway to the weekend, it seems to promise relief from all that has worn and torn us in our work. Yet in spite of frequent weekends, holidays, and paid vacations, a satisfying rest seems to escape many people. To them "blue Monday" symbolizes the reluctant return to the harness. Employers who continually cope with the problem of Monday absenteeism know that in spite of the two-day break many of their employees are still in no shape to return to profitable work.

The human heart longs after a lasting rest, one that will carry us through the work week. Our need and desire is not simply time off to escape work responsibilities, but time off to allow the battle-wounds of the week to heal, to reorient ourselves and regain an inner harmony. Serenity. Rest. Peace. But how can we who run in the "rat race" of the workaday world stop long enough to find them and make them our own?

As might be expected, the Scriptures are not silent on a subject of such universal importance to human beings. For rest is not an invention of man. God Himself took the first rest. "And by the seventh day God completed His work which He had done; and He rested on the seventh day from all His work which He had done" (Genesis 2: 2). Here, as in work, the heavenly pattern was set. God worked: therefore man works. God rested: therefore man rests. In the Fourth Commandment God instructed the Israelites to work six days and then to cease working on the seventh. Why? "For in six days the Lord made the heavens and the earth, the sea and all that is in them, and rested on the seventh day; therefore the Lord blessed the sabbath day and made it holy" (Exodus 20: 11).

Although we Christians are not encumbered with all the rules and regulations of the Jewish Sabbath, we should not lightly disregard God's own example. The legal sabbath-keeping requirement was a "mere shadow of what is to come," yet the heavenly pattern still stands. God, the Creator who never sleeps (Psalm 121: 4), worked six days and "was refreshed" by a cessation of labor on the seventh day (Exodus 31: 17). How much more does man, the sleep-dependent creature who tires so quickly, also require a day of refreshment and rest. God put His breath of life into beings who easily become fatigued. Jesus recognized this fact when He said to sleepy-eyed Peter: ". . . the spirit is willing, but the flesh is weak" (Mark 14: 38). God knows that our work wears us out. He remembers that we are made of dust. And so He has provided certain "rest areas" along life's highway where that which has been worn by our labor may be repaired.

One such rest area is the day we sometimes call the Lord's day. Although under no legal obligation to do so, most Christians today observe Sunday as a day of rest, at least to one extent or another. Sunday thus provides a physical rest for the body, when the daily work can be laid aside for a whole 24-hour period. Some Christians believe they should do absolutely no work on Sundays. Others see nothing wrong with certain activities, claiming that they find rest in this way. Neither group should condemn the other (Romans 14: 5, 6, 13). But it should be remembered that the heavenly pattern sets aside one day for a rest from the work of the other six days. God's six-to-one work-rest ratio has been written into the order of things. Originally it included not only man but also animals (Deuteronomy 5: 14), and even the land (Leviticus 25: 1–6). The closer we order our ways of working according to God's ways of working, the more fruitful our work will become.

Not only has God given us one day in seven to rest, but He has also given us the night hours in which to rest our bodies from work. The darkness provides yet another rest area. By hiding the sun God originally made it almost impossible to work at night. But today, under electric lights, we are no longer limited to daylight hours for working. Unfortunately, some who are driven by their work feel that the hours spent in bed are a waste of time. By simply flicking a switch, so it seems, we ought to be able to work night and day. Some Christians have felt uneasy on this score. They have suspected that rest and sleep were somehow a giving in to the desires of the body. Such people have difficulty in reconciling sleep with the Scripture which tells us to redeem the time and to make the best possible use of it.

But there is nothing wrong with feeling fatigue or resting our bodies. The Gospels picture Jesus as growing tired in His body and taking time out to rest. "Jesus therefore, being wearied from His journey, was sitting thus by the well" (John 4: 6). In another place, during a boat trip, Jesus "was in the stern, asleep on the cushion . . ." (Mark 4: 38). After a particularly busy time Jesus invited His disciples to "Come away by yourselves to a lonely place and rest a while" (Mark 6: 31). In this particular instance their plans for a vacation were interrupted by a crowd of needy people. We see, though, that Jesus cares about the physical, bodily well-being of His followers and that He recognizes our need for rest periods. Yes, even a vacation may be the best possible use of our time. Only a properly rested body will be fully ready for the demands of work which God will place upon it.

God has so ordered it that certain days and hours are to be set aside for rest and sleep to remedy our body weariness. But there is another kind of weariness, soul weariness, which cannot be healed through sleep or relaxation. Soul weariness can actually rob us of sleep. At times body weariness can have a certain pleasantness about it—it makes rest and sleep so peaceful, so well deserved. But soul weariness is something else again. Soul weariness involves tension, the disturbing of our inner peace, the deep unrest of mind and heart which saps strength from the vital center of our being. Body weariness may be relieved through rest days and sleep at night. But soul weariness requires a more constant rest, not just intermittent relief. Has God provided any rest area for our soul weariness?

Jesus has promised: "Come to Me, all who are weary and heavy laden, and I will give you rest. Take My yoke upon you, and learn from Me, for I am gentle and humble in heart; and you shall find *rest for your souls*" (Matthew 11: 28, 29). Jesus promises us rest for our souls. Vicious conflicts rage in the soul. Satan fights against us there. As David put it, ". . . the enemy has persecuted my soul; he has crushed my life to the ground . . ." (Psalm 143: 3). Our own desires battle against us here. Peter wrote of keeping ourselves from "fleshly lusts, which wage war against the soul" (1 Peter 2: 11). Paul found that the "law of sin" in the members of his body waged war against that higher law which his mind knew to be right and good (Romans 7: 23).

This is the war that wearies the soul, this struggling to do the right and being overpowered by the wrong. Our daily work is one thing; it can tire us. But far more exhausting is the work of fighting sin in our own strength. The Christian who works in the world knows he should not hate the fellow worker who won the promotion through deceit. He struggles and works against his resentment. But in spite of all his efforts, it rises up and overwhelms him. He knows he should not look with desire at the short-skirted secretary, and he fights mightily against it. But even if he turns away the physical eye he finds the picture in his imagination. He knows that rumor about the boss should not be passed along and bites his tongue to keep it back—only to realize too late that it has slipped out inadvertently. This war wears out the soul. Where in the working world can the soul find peace and an end to its war?

Soul rest won't be found in the world. It comes only as a gift from above. Jesus said, "I will *give* you rest." This is why the world fails to find rest for its soul weariness: lacking faith, the non-Christian is unable to receive God's gifts. "There is no peace for the wicked" (Isaiah 48: 22). The world searches for soul rest in all the wrong places—in sports, recreation, hobbies, music, alcohol, or drugs, to name just a few. But true peace of heart and mind is a gift from the Prince of Peace. It has no other source. As Jesus said, "Peace I leave with you; My peace I give to you; not as the world gives, do I give to you. Let not your heart be troubled, nor let it be fearful" (John 14: 27).

In any war the losing side is bound to be fearful. So it is in our soul's war. We work against sin, yet it defeats us. Soon we learn to fear the sin, dreading its power and knowing our own weakness. The fear adds to the intensity of our inner turmoil. That is why the promise of divine rest becomes so attractive. The writer of the Book of Hebrews, in speaking of the "sabbath rest" which is open to

God's people today, stated that ". . . the one who has entered His rest has himself also rested from his works, as God did from His" (Hebrews 4: 10). In other words, when we receive the gift of God's rest we may rest from all our hard working at trying to overcome sin with our own goodness. Jesus, by His bodily life, death, bloodshed, and resurrection, overpowered it. He mastered sin. That which had proved too strong for us was no match for Him. Now He wants to share with us the benefits gained by His victory. He wants to give us rest and peace. In Him our inner war can come to an end!

Think of our situation as similar to that of a small boy troubled by the neighborhood bully. Each time he ventures outside to play or go to school, the bully pounces on him and gives him a good beating. Naturally, after several such encounters, the little boy lives in constant fear. But suppose the boy's father promises him that he will always walk with him wherever he goes. The father, larger and stronger than the bully, has no fear of walking about. He walks in rest and peace. And his son, though weak in himself, can enter into his father's rest by simply trusting his father to deliver him from the bully. In the same way we, through trusting in Jesus' promise never to leave us, can enter into His rest. As God told Moses, "My presence shall go with you, and I will give you rest" (Exodus 33: 14).

Faith in what God has promised is the only pathway into true rest. Unbelief will prevent us, like it did the ancient Jews, from entering God's rest. But even the way of faith has its learning process. Jesus has invited us to take His yoke upon us and to *learn* from Him. What lessons can we working people learn from Him that will help us to find rest? Jesus, after extending the invitation to come and learn from Him, added, "for I am gentle and humble in heart." Among the outstanding "unworldly" character traits of Jesus is humble-heartedness. The dictionary defines the word "humble" as "not proud or haughty, not arrogant or assertive, ranking low in some hierarchy or scale, insignificant." What does humility have to do with rest?

Those of us who work in Babylon know that the kingdom of this world doesn't run on humility. The world has been overrun by an enemy who has lied to us by making it appear that we must lift ourselves into significance, that we must try to "be somebody." The kingdom set up by Satan, the enemy ruler, stands in stark contrast to the kingdom of God. Humble-heartedness, insignificance, low rank —seemingly these will get you nowhere in terms of the kingdom of this world. The enemy ruler has made it appear that greatness in his kingdom will be achieved through climbing a ladder, the rungs being wealth, praise from the mouths of men, positions of power and influence, and skin-deep good appearances. From this ladder Babylon the Great is being built. The enemy ruler never lacks those who will promote his propaganda. We who work are told we should assert ourselves. We are branded as lacking in initiative if we do not engage in the struggle for the top positions. In some circles, to be overworked is a status symbol. Higher salaries are dangled, carrot-like, in front of us. In a thousand ways we are urged to push, struggle, strain, strive, and sweat to "realize our potential," to "fulfill" ourselves.

The person who enters the world of work faces the danger of becoming enmeshed in the enemy ruler's scheme. Once trapped, he will come to loathe the bottom rung and lust after the top. He becomes afraid of missing his potential, of failure to elevate himself into something worthwhile. He pursues a salary increase. Having got it he finds himself envying those who earn even more. He gets promoted to a higher position. Once there his eyes open to the possibility of yet a loftier one. He fears being seen as insignificant in the eyes of the world. Driven by this fear, he strives to at least *appear* successful, even if the reality of it is missing from his heart. What a load to carry! Is it any wonder that Jesus described it as a burden?

We inherited a proud and sinful heart from our first parents. Left to ourselves, to our natural impulses, we would be forever drawn to the enemy's ladder because it has irresistible power to attract the flesh. But Jesus, through His death and blood sacrifice, has broken that magnetic attraction of sin. He now offers to take us off the enemy ruler's ladder to phony greatness and to put us on God's ladder to true greatness—with the assurance that at the end of the climb we'll find fullness, not emptiness.

But at first glance it appears that "up is down" on God's ladder, and we shy away from it. The world tells us: "Fulfill yourself." But God says: "Empty yourself." Then He promises to fill us with His own Spirit. "Have this attitude in yourselves which was also in Christ Jesus, who . . . emptied Himself, taking the form of a bondservant. . . . He humbled Himself . . . . Therefore also God highly exalted Him, and bestowed on Him the name which is above every name . . ." (Philippians 2: 5–9). Christ took the low place, the humble place, and God lifted Him up to a high position. Each Christian should follow Christ's pattern as he works in the world. Scripture promises: "Humble yourselves in the presence of the Lord, and He will exalt you" (James 4: 10). There is a ladder to greatness in God's kingdom—and the way up *is* down.

The working world tells us: "Struggle to realize your potential." But God says, "You are already complete in Christ." As Christians engaged in ordinary work we may find real rest in the assurance that ". . . in Him [Christ] all the fulness of Diety dwells in bodily form, and in Him you have been made complete . . ." (Colossians 2: 9, 10). There are, of course, areas in these earthly bodies which still must be brought into conformity with Christ's life. But as we abide in Christ, we find Him to be our completeness. Our frantic search for significance ends in Him. In Christ we are significant. As a member of His Body, each of us is a vital organ.

The world tells us: "Drive yourself. Get that promotion. Impress everyone with your position." But the humble-hearted Jesus shows us a different way. "You know," He said, "that the rulers of the Gentiles lord it over them, and their great men exercise authority over them. It is not so among you, but whoever wishes to become great among you shall be your servant, and whoever wishes to be first among you shall be your slave" (Matthew 20: 25–27). Jesus is not saying here that the world should not have persons in authority, nor is He saying that God's people should never occupy such positions. No, He is saying that true greatness comes by humbly serving others, not by outranking them. We are not to seek after position to make ourselves great. We are to seek God's greatness by giving ourselves in humble service to our fellow men. He will see to it that we are placed in positions where that service can most effectively be performed.

The world tells us: "Keep pushing for higher pay. Save up money, build security for your old age." But God's Word to us is far different. He calls us to a life of giving away and sharing, then promises to supply all our needs.

As we compare the world's message with Jesus' message, it is obvious which will be more restful. The world's way involves self-struggle, possessiveness, and pretense. God's way means letting Him fight for us, being openhanded and generous with our possessions, and being exactly what we appear to be. When Jesus said that His yoke was easy and His burden light, He meant easy and light in comparison with the yoke and burden imposed by the enemy ruler. And He said that by choosing to learn from Him, we will find rest for our soul weariness.

How do we who work learn Jesus' way? It all comes down to a matter of believing Him or not believing Him. If we actually trust Him to supply our needs instead of setting about to supply our own needs through self-effort, we will find Him true to His Word. In practice, we're going to believe either the enemy ruler or the rightful Ruler. Both make promises. Satan promises great rewards for self-effort, but acting on his promise leads to soul weariness, emptiness, and death. When we have stopped trusting our own working and begin relying on God's promise to work in us and for us, then we enter His rest, a rest which can be ours every day of the week, not just one day out of seven.

The lies of the enemy ruler which cause unrest do not all come from what the world tells us. Some our unrest springs from our own flesh. Many men are motivated to work harder simply to prevent a co-worker from getting ahead of them. Competition in sports and games is child's play compared to the competition which can develop in the work world. Solomon saw this: "And I have seen that every labor and every skill which is done is the result of rivalry between a man and his neighbor. This too is vanity and striving after wind" (Ecclesiastes 4: 4).

Many of us relish competition between man and man. The flesh gains a sweet satisfaction in having triumphed over a rival, whether in basketball or business. This is rooted in our urge to elevate ourselves, to prove "number one" better than all comers. But God tells us not to think of ourselves more highly than we ought to think—even to consider others better than ourselves. James put it this way: ". . . if you have bitter jealousy and selfish ambition in your heart, do not be arrogant and so lie against the truth. This wisdom is not that which comes down from above, but is earthly, natural, demonic. For where jealousy and selfish ambition exist, there is disorder and every evil thing. But the wisdom from above is first pure, then peaceable, gentle, reasonable, full of mercy and good fruits, unwavering, without hypocrisy. And the seed whose fruit is righteousness is sown in peace by those who make peace" (James 3: 14–18.) And peace, remember, is rest. Rivalry destroys soul rest.

There is yet another source of unrest in our work, one that may surprise us. We are prepared to accept the fact that unrest can come from the world, our own flesh, or the devil. But we may not have recognized the unrest that can spring from our religious training. Tension can be produced by trying to follow religious teachings which are said to be God's Word, but which are actually slight twistings of God's Word. When Jesus said the Jewish religious leaders "tie up heavy loads, and lay them on men's shoulders" (Matthew 23: 4), He was referring to the man-made traditions and the seemingly harmless additions to God's Word with which they burdened the people. We must be very careful here. An authentic word from God, if properly received, liberates. But the effects of man-made teaching are to bring men into bondage (Colossians 2: 8). Such bondage unsettles the soul.

The whole gamut of subtle ways in which the non-clerical person gets the message "You're just a layman" can produce unrest. We meet saints in the New Testament, but no "laymen." The term, though widely used, has come from man-made traditions. Unrest can result from the false division between sacred and secular. If only such activities as witnessing, teaching a Sunday school class, singing in the choir, and repairing the church building are the work of God, then we will feel an unease about any other kind of work. But if, as Scripture urges us, we do everything heartily, as to the Lord, we will find rest.

Sometimes we who work in ordinary jobs get tensed up

because we aren't seeing the results of our labor. Those who work for Christian organizations find a certain measure of comfort in counting. By working within the limits of a well-defined group and particular programs, such people can compare this year's attendance with last year's, can add up the number of hours spent in counseling, can tell you how many hospital or prison visits were made, how many converts came forward last month, and how many will be baptized next Sunday.

But the man who works in the world cannot so easily gain visible assurances of his influence. He serves not a denomination nor an organization, but the Body of Christ. Who can tell how many other Christians have been encouraged and built up by the power of his example? How can he number the times he has, knowingly or unknowingly, offered counsel? Who can measure the influence exerted by his habit of forgiving his enemies and rivals on the job and by his spending time in prayer for them? Such a man must, by faith, believe that God is using him as long as he remains abiding in Christ. Now and then he may receive some "feedback" which will encourage him. But he must operate, in the main, with few tangible evidences of his effectiveness. And he must be able to rest content with this. Otherwise he may be caught up in a frenzy of religious activity in a desperate search for visible signs of achievement in spiritual things.

How, then, shall we who work expect to find rest? Like the world we will have our Fridays and our paid vacations. These we will use as God directs, but we will not expect our soul rest from them. Instead, we will look above for our rest, expecting it as a gift from the Savior. We will stop looking to the world, even the religious world, for our satisfaction and rewards. We will stop trying to struggle for the top spots through our own efforts, and will adopt the attitude of the Christian employee who said: "I've finally realized I don't *have* to be president."

By what signs will you recognize the gift of God's rest when it comes? It comes in gentleness and quietness, even in the thick of busyness and bustle all about. Jesus' rest will make you glad to be right where you are—because wherever you are, He is. The spirit of hurry will be gone when Jesus rests you. Yes, you may at times work or move rapidly, but not because you are being driven to it by some inner struggle. If you are traveling in a car, you will be content to be exactly where you are, without wishing you'd already arrived. If you rank low on some organizational "totem pole," you will find yourself thanking God for your place, because He has assigned you there. If your salary is lower than that of many around you, you will be "free from the love of money, being content with what you have; for He Himself has said, 'I will never desert you, nor will I ever forsake you' " (Hebrews 13: 5). How shall we recognize God's rest? In God's rest we will find our comfort and delight in Him alone. In His rest our highest delight is to live and work every day in company with Him.

Baruch, who served as secretary to Jeremiah, the prophet, apparently knew the tension of expecting too much from this world. He had said: "Ah, woe is me! For the Lord has added sorrow to my pain; I am weary with my groaning and have found no rest" (Jeremiah 45: 3). Through Jeremiah, God had to remind Baruch of the fact that what he saw in the world was only to last a short time and then would be gone. Then God said to Baruch: "But you, are you seeking great things for yourself? Do not seek them . . ." (v. 5).

In seeking great things from the world for ourselves we will find only sorrow, pain, unrest. But in humbly seeking first God's kingdom and His righteousness (which is Christ), we will be gifted with rest from above. Jesus gave easy-to-follow directions for reaching the rest area for our souls: "Come to Me. . . ," He said. The soul's rest area is in Him. By coming to Him, abiding in Him, and learning from Him, you will experience His promised rest. Many highway rest areas are posted, "No overnight camping." But Jesus invites you to stay in His rest area forever—even on Mondays!

11

THE CHURCH IN THE WORKPLACE

THE SCRIPTURES TEACH that our everyday jobs are immensely important in God's sight. Each Christian, as a priest, is to become a minister of God in the place where he lives and works. In this way the Church daily invades the world's darkness with its light. But a knowledge of various on-the-job ministries will not be enough. Unless we also obtain from God His vision of the Church, we will be hindered in our efforts to function consistently as priests in ordinary work clothes.

If we find that the expression of Christ's life is less than it ought to be in the lives of Christians who work in the world, it is possible that a part of the problem lies in a faulty conception of the Church. Many causes of weakness may be traced to individual failure. But corporate failure, too, can limit the expression of Christ's life on earth. Has a deficient view of the Church led many of us into blind alleys in which we see no way to "really serve the Lord" in our jobs? Is our church structure built according to the heavenly pattern? Or have we followed human traditions in our attempts to build up the Church?

Why should we even bother considering church framework and structure? In earlier chapters it was emphasized that Christ's *life* is the light of men. Since it is only this spiritual life from above that can produce light, why concern ourselves with framework and structure? The answer should be evident: wherever we look, life expresses itself through structure and form. Corn life invariably exhibits itself through the structure of the cornstalk. Rabbit life always comes in a furry framework. The human body is the only package that expresses life in *Homo sapiens.* Only through structure and form can life display itself on earth.

What form or structure expresses the life of Christ on earth? Paul asked the Corinthian believers, "Do you not know that your body is a temple of the Holy Spirit who is in you . . . ?" (1 Corinthians 6: 19). We see, then, that Christ's life exhibits itself through individual human bodies. But no single human body on earth today can provide a framework large enough to express fully the life of Christ. Each of us, individually, can contain only a small portion of Christ's life. It is in the Church, the Body of Christ, that Christ's life is expressed in its full measure. God has made Christ "head over all things to the church, which is *His body, the fullness of Him* who fills all in all" (Ephesians 1: 22, 23). If we would see the life of Christ expressed in its fullness on earth, we must look not to the individual body but to the Church, the corporate Body of Christ.

The Body of Christ, as God sees it, is composed of the true Christians who make up its various members, each with differing roles and functions. Crowning all is the supreme member of the Body, its directing member, Christ Himself, who is its Head. God recognizes our individuality, our uniqueness as members (or organs) of the Body of Christ. But He also sees that the health of any member in a body, even in the Body of Christ, depends to a great extent on the health of the rest of the body. For example, a "root of bitterness" in one individual member of Christ's Body is not just that individual's problem: it may pollute many members (Hebrews 12: 15).

It follows, then, that the only accurate way to view each Christian who works in an ordinary job is in relationship to his or her setting within the above context. We cannot really understand an individual Christian without understanding his or her place within the Body of Christ. For example, suppose I ask a doctor why my hand will not grasp properly. Will he examine only my hand? No—he'll probably also inspect many other bodily members which affect it. The real problem may be in my arm. In the same way, each Christian who works in the world is helped or hindered by the other members of Christ's Body around him. To diagnose his condition requires a close look, not only at him as an individual, but also at the Christian community surrounding him, at the structure which supports him.

Structure, therefore, becomes very important. Only the Spirit of God can bring the life from heaven to earth through the words of God, but that life must find the proper structure for its full expression. Right structure cannot produce life, but wrong structure can hinder the expression of life. Putting elephant life into mouse structure would greatly thwart the expression of elephant life!

A similar thwarting occurs when we attempt to substitute something other than the Body of Christ as the structure for expressing His life before the world. We may establish an organization, and may even call it "church." But if its structure is other than the structure of the Body of Christ, as revealed in Scripture, then the thing that we have built will only hinder the full manifestation of Christ's life.

The imprecise way in which we have come to use the word "church" can cloud our vision here. In the New Testament the word has one basic meaning: "called out" or "summoned forth." When the New Testament writers used the word "church" in reference to the Body of Christ, they made only two specific applications of this basic meaning. The first application was to the universal Church, the great assembly of God's called-out ones, past, present, and future, which will one day gather around His throne to worship Him. The second application was limited by time and place: thus, the local church includes all God's called-out ones in a given community at a particular point in time (i.e., the Church in Antioch, the Church in Jerusalem, the Church in Corinth, etc.). Without exception in Scripture, a local church included all the believers in that community.

Today, however, we recognize many human additions to the meaning of the word. We apply the term "church" to the meetingplace, to the wood or stone building in which believers assemble. We apply the word "church" to describe a particular congregation or assembly of believers which does not include all the called-out ones in that particular community. We use the word "church" to mean a denominational organization (i.e., the "Baptist church," the "Presbyterian church," the "Catholic church"). By using the word in this way we suggest that there is not one Church in a given community, but many. Yet the New Testament knows only one Church per community. We also employ "church" to describe something larger than a denomination, yet smaller than the universal Church, when we talk of the "evangelical church," or the "liberal church," or the "orthodox church."

What difference does it make how we use the word "church"? For one thing, we never quite know what someone else means when he uses the word. I may speak to you using the word "church" in reference to all the believers in our community, but you may take me to mean the building at the corner of Seventh and Main in which we regularly assemble on Sundays. Worse, we both may read in the

Scriptures that we are to use our various giftings to build up the "Church," and interpret this to mean that our responsibility is simply to minister to the believers in our own congregation or assembly. Through wrong use of the word, our eyes may be blinded to our responsibility to build up the believers near us on the job, yet who worship with other groups. Our usage of scriptural words must correspond with scriptural meaning, for "if the bugle produces an indistinct sound, who will prepare himself for battle?" (1 Corinthians 14: 8). Any misuse of the word "church" according to our own ideas may contribute to the building up of a structure not of God's design.

Using the term "church" in ways not found in Scripture can lead to an inability to discern the true Church, God's household. This inability causes many to falter. They grope along in defeat and confusion. There seems to be no relationship between what happens in church on Sunday to what happens weekdays on the job. "Church" is seen to be something separate from life. From the perspective of the ordinary job, "church" seems to be "out there," located blocks or miles away in a building set apart for God's work. But such a view only fosters the division of life into mutually exclusive sacred and secular parts. In God's sight I am as fully in Church on the job as I am when assembled with other Christians in the meetingplace on Sunday. The Church is neither a place nor an event. It is the Body of Christ. Christ's Body does not shift into a state of suspended animation when the benediction is pronounced after the Sunday morning sermon. His Body, like any human body, is continually functioning, even when seemingly at rest. When a Christian reports to work Monday morning, the Church shows up there with him.

Wrong use of the word "church" can also blind us to the need of our Christian groups to "die" to the self-life. At first the thought of a corporate "death-to-self" may seem strange. Normally we think in terms of individual self-denial. We have grown accustomed to applying the New Testament passages on crucifying the self-life to ourselves on a one-by-one basis. But we may have overlooked our need to apply these same passages to our groups as well. Any group, like the individuals who compose it, develops certain appetites and desires. It comes with its own self-life, drawing its energies from the fleshly life which Jesus said should be lost (Luke 9: 24) and hated (Luke 14: 26). As time passes this corporate self-life and its drives often intensify, just as many desires of the flesh tend to increase with age in individuals. What are some of our collective desires of the flesh?

Rivalry is one. We like to believe "our group" is just a bit superior to those other gatherings. Our doctrine is several shades purer, we display more missionary zeal, we're not as fanatical, or we practice a more biblical form of baptism. In countless ways we can manage to rate ourselves on top in any comparison. Yet Scripture tells us as individuals that each of us is to "regard one another as more important than himself " (Philippians 2: 3). Certainly we are not to follow another standard on the *group* level!

Enlargement can become another corporate desire of the flesh. If we are better than other groups, we should also be bigger. So we devise a variety of methods to increase attendance and add to the membership list. Usually we cloak all these efforts with very admirable explanations of our intent. But hidden out of sight can be other motives: to impress or triumph over other congregations; to gain a sense of accomplishment for our efforts; to satisfy and please the growth-conscious heads of a denomination in some distant city. For it is true that the corporate heart, like the individual heart, is "desperately sick" (Jeremiah 17: 9).

Self-preservation could be added to the list of corporate lusts. As individuals we are prone to reject whatever threatens us—even constructive criticism. Collectively, too, we cringe at any suggestion that we have failed in this area or that.

The love of money is a problem not only among individuals. It can also taint our corporate vision. When a group begins to acquire things, its possessions beget more possessions. Buildings and property and equipment and programs soon develop their own healthy hungers for funds. It becomes far too easy for the owning group to become the "owned" group.

These are just four examples of fleshly desires which can subtly infiltrate our groups. The list could be made much longer. Scripture tells us that the desires of the flesh are at war with our souls as individuals. Our corporate lusts war against our groups in the same way that they war against us individually—they make us self-centered. Unless a group consistently dies to its corporate lusts of the flesh, the group will become more concerned with its own welfare and survival than with serving the needs of the larger Body of Christ. Any group which refuses to "fall into the ground and die" to itself, will soon become self-serving. This is not to say that we should abandon our groups any more than we should abandon any member of our bodies of flesh. The point is that we recognize and deny self, whether self appears on the individual or corporate level.

During the days of Jesus' earthly life the Pharisees were one group that refused to die to their collective desires of the flesh. They believed themselves to be better than other groups and classes of men (Luke 18: 9–12; John 9: 34). They went to great lengths to enlarge their numbers (Matthew 23: 15). To preserve themselves and their status quo they used fear of expulsion from their group (John 9:

22; 12: 42). And it was apparently common knowledge that this group loved money (Luke 16: 14). The Pharisees were those who seemingly held the Scriptures in highest regard. Yet they had become self-serving to such a degree that they and their teachings brought people into bondage rather than into God's liberty. In choosing to serve and preserve the self-life of the Pharisee community, they forfeited any capacity to serve God and other men. Ultimately, of course, this refusal to die to themselves led them to demand the death of Jesus. Jesus' teachings forced them to choose: either death to the corporate lusts of their own group, or death to the body of Jesus. In order to save their own "life," the Pharisees saw clearly that Jesus' body must die.

In a way we face the same choice today. If the Church, the Body of Christ, is to live, we must die to our individual self-interests and those of our groups. We have inherited an "institutional church" which has strayed far from God's intent. He has indicated plainly that the Church in each community is one. Yet we present the world with a picture of division into hundreds of sects and denominations. Each of these groups can be deceived by its corporate lusts of the flesh. Each faces the constant danger of becoming self-serving and self-preserving.

You and I did not originate the divisions and denominations. We may even feel trapped by them. But what can we do? We see the folly of running off to start another sect and of pronouncing it to be "The True Church." Yet there is another way. There is no need to abandon our present groups, unless God's Spirit should distinctly so lead. The real need is vision: we need to *see* our group as simply part of the one Church in our community. We must *see* that in our community there is only one Church—though it may have many meeting places. Group A and Group B are not "churches" in themselves. Rather, they are gatherings, assemblies, congregations of Christ's followers. Group A and Group B should not meet to build up their own separate groups. Instead, they should meet to build up the Body of Christ in the whole community. As the Body of Christ grows, so will the individual groups within it. But in order for this to happen, both Group A and Group B must be in a continual process of "dying" to themselves.

This corporate death will prove to be painful. It will require sacrifice. It will require dependence upon God's strength instead of the group's natural strength. We will have to learn the costly work of equipping men to follow Christ in the context of their ordinary jobs, without expecting these men to "repay" us through heavy involvement in programs centered about our meeting place. We will have to learn ways to increase the visible unity and fellowship between the various congregations in our community. We will have to learn to receive group correction, both from individuals within our own group and from other groups. We may even be called upon to send a new believer over to another group which may be better suited to meet his unique needs. This corporate dying may involve financial help to other groups in our community. It may mean learning how to place the needs of the poor above the needs of our buildings, our equipment, and our programs. Most importantly, we will have to learn how to train our people to see the difference between serving the Body of Christ and serving our own group.

Time after time we should ask God to search us with the question: "In which specific areas are You calling our group to 'die' to itself? What will it mean for our assembly of believers to deny itself?" Only in such a structure, in a "dying" group of Christians, can its members who work in the world fully express the life of Christ. But if a group refuses to put to death its collective self-life, the man who works in an ordinary job will find the group's demands draining him, *feeding upon* him instead of *feeding* him. The group will demand his time, his talent, and his money to build itself—perhaps even labeling this as service to the Body of Christ. As these demands grow, he will find his spiritual strength sapped, weakening his life and light before the world.

An ordinary job has little value to the self-life of a group. Pumping gas can't serve the corporate self-interest of any congregation very far. It may of course provide one more source of income for the group, or it may be seen as a hunting-ground for new members. But for the most part, if Christians adjust their priorities in terms of their group's self-life, they will assign a low price tag to everday work. In this framework the expression of Christ's life is limited in the one who works in the world.

But within the framework of the Body of Christ, ordinary work is of immense value. It affords us a lampstand from which Christ's light in us may shine, bringing praise to God. It provides God with countless opportunities to shape us into Christ's likeness. Our work allows us to minister God's grace to other believers who work near us on the job. It enables us to share our faith with unbelievers. And it allows us to participate in carrying out God's first command, to subdue and rule over the earth and its creatures. May all of us ask God for a greater vision of the Body of Christ and serve it instead of our own group's ends. Only in His Body can Christ's life be fully displayed before a watching world.

12

HELP WANTED: SPIRITUAL GROWNUPS

WE WHO WORK IN THE WORLD need to see the same Church that God sees. Beyond that we must also have God's vision of the task of the Church. Unless we see clearly the work He has assigned to the Church, how will we recognize what will be required to accomplish that work?

Paul, the apostle, had as clear a conception of the work of the Church as any man. He said that the whole point of his labor in preaching, warning, and teaching was "that we may present every man complete [mature] in Christ" (Colossians 1: 28). Although the Galatian Christians were "all sons of God through faith in Christ Jesus" (Galatians 3: 26), Paul underwent spiritual labor pains until Christ was formed in them (4: 19).

In his letter to the Church at Ephesus Paul further clarified the task of the Church: "And He gave some as apostles, and some as prophets, and some as evangelists, and some as pastors and teachers, for the equipping of the saints for the work of the service, to the building up of the body of Christ; until we all attain to the unity of the faith, and of the knowledge of the Son of God, to a mature man, to the measure of the stature which belongs to the fulness of Christ. As a result, we are no longer to be children . . .". (Ephesians 4: 11–14).

God has set His heart on people of spiritual maturity, people who have attained not only oneness with Himself, but also oneness with all other Christians around them—a people who corporately express the fullness which is found in Christ. Converting sinners and bringing them into unity and full maturity, this is the task of the church.

What does maturity look like? What sort of believers should we be trying to produce? After spending five or ten years in our group, what should be the result in the lives of individuals who work in the world?

There seem to be many answers proposed for this question. Some apparently believe that real maturity is reflected when one leaves ordinary work to enter gospel work. Carrying this view to its logical conclusion would mean that an "ideal" congregation would produce nothing but ministers, missionaries, youth workers, evangelists, etc. But Scripture does not indicate that the church is to aim at the mass-production of gospel workers.

God does need gospel workers, but the gifting and appointment of these men is His work. The work of the church is to make disciples (learners) and to teach them all that Jesus commanded. The aim of the church is to produce vital, healthy followers of Christ. A Christian properly trained to follow Him will then be ready to hear His voice—whether the call be into ordinary work or gospel work.

Another idea seems to be that the church succeeds when it produces a believer who can recite certain formulas for salvation. Many efforts are aimed at the turning out of those who can deliver pre-packaged outlines to non-Christians. Is this really our object? Do we want "religious parrots" who have the words embedded in their memory cells, but whose lives show little evidence of those words having become flesh? Are theologically correct words all we owe to the world?

Scripture tells us that we should "Owe nothing to anyone except to love one another; for he who loves his neighbor has fulfilled the law" (Romans 13: 8). We should be producing lovers-of-men, not mere talkers-to-men. He who knows how to love will find the right words. But it is not always true in reverse. If we have simply produced a Christian who can mouth a formula, how will he know when to speak and when to remain silent? How will he tailor his words to the unique needs of the person to whom he is talking? But if we have produced a Christian who loves, he will know when silence is appropriate and when speech will serve best.

Again, we should look to our pattern. Jesus never resorted to the use of a formula in His contacts with sinners. Each new encounter brought a fresh response from Jesus. His words were not "canned," they did not flow from His memory. His words flowed from the very center of a Person who loved God and man with total love. It could well be said of Christ Himself that "his mouth speaks from that which fills his heart" (Luke 6: 45). If Jesus' words proceeded from a love-filled heart, and if we are to make disciples for Him, then we must produce men whose hearts are full of love. We can be confident that any outflow of words will be right if the heart is right.

What kind of mature believers are we aiming for? Some groups, apparently, want to produce Christians who simply function well in terms of their own particular program. Have we achieved success when we can point to a Christian who never misses a meeting? Have we reached our goal when each person is "programmed" into the organizational structure of things? Is the "ideal Christian" one who never questions the directions his group is taking, who will accept without serious examination whatever the leadership teaches or suggests? If this is the sort of "maturity" we're after, we had better examine our motives.

A group which measures the spiritual stature of its members in terms of their involvement in choir practice, teachers' meetings, and the building program has all the symptoms of corporate self-service. We have already noted the collective "self-life" which threatens groups of believers. It is this group urge which desires to capture the time and efforts of individuals *for its own use.* We must be very careful here. It is God's desire that individuals serve the Body of Christ. And it is also His plan that some of this service should take place through organized groups. But it is not His plan to have an individual's talents or gifts used to promote the self-life of any congregation.

Groups, like individuals, tend to imitate and copy one another. In our minds, a Christian gathering just isn't "church" unless there is a sermon, a choir, Sunday school classes for all ages, greeters, ushers, and a pianist or organist. Thus, there are certain "holes" in the organizational structure which must be filled before we are satisfied. Corporate pressure is exerted whenever there are vacancies.

Richard Halverson wrote: "The church has succeeded in pulling Christians out of the world—out of society—out of community and civic affairs. So often it is a little island of irrelevant piety surrounded by an ocean of need. And our preoccupation with the establishment has been so complete that we have been unable to see the ocean . . . except, of course, if there is someone out there that we want to recruit for the program. The congregation has become an exclusive little system of satellites orbiting around the program . . ." *(Relevance).*

How much better it would be if we were to design our programs around what God has given us, rather than to force our people into preconceived programs. Let's ask God to show us the various giftings He has placed among us. And let's ask Him why He has done so. Then, having recognized the abilities and gifts God has placed among us at the moment, and having understood why we need this particular "mix" at this time, we can proceed to design any needed programs. Otherwise, we will find ourselves plugging round holes with square pegs and wondering why our programs won't hold water.

But even a properly designed program is only a means, not the goal. Since most Christians spend the major part of their time in ordinary work, our real goal should be to produce mature Christians who can take their places as lights in this dark world. We should be equipping believers with sufficient vision and power to transform their ordinary jobs into service to God and to man.

We need people in gospel work. We need people who will carry out certain organized efforts and programs within our groups. But why are such people needed? Not to perpetuate programs, but to prepare Christians to live the Christ-life out in the world. Attendance at church meetings and participation in church-related events are neither the ends nor the measures of maturity. A man should not be made to feel he is failing God if his schedule does not allow him perfect attendance, or if his calling does not include leadership in programs which center around the meeting place. Our goal is to equip him for a ministry *in terms of his life,* not in terms of our program.

None of us should make a habit of "forsaking our own assembling together" (Hebrews 10: 25). But we should always remember that the point of assembling as Christians is to "stimulate one another to love and good deeds" and to encourage one another (vv. 24, 25). Jesus recognized not only the large gatherings, but also the very small ones. He said, "For where two or three have gathered together in My name, there I am in their midst" (Matthew 18: 20). Who can deny that this is a Church meeting? The Head of the Body and some members.

What more is needed to constitute a genuine gathering of the Church?

I can attend a Church meeting during a coffee break or lunch hour by getting together with one or two other Christians in the name of Jesus. This is not to imply that we should neglect the larger gatherings. They, too, are extremely important to our growth. But why content ourselves with only two or three Church meetings a week? Hundreds of these small meetings can take place every week in our communities and work places, each with the promised presence of the Head of the Body. One Body, many meeting places.

The real question, then, is not "How involved is the man in our program?" but "How well is our program equipping him for the roles God has assigned to him?" How fruitful is this man in terms of his God-given position within the Body of Christ? Does this man do his everyday work as to the Lord and not for men? Is he obedient to his employer? Is his work becoming a false god in his life? Does he have a full or only a partial vision of his daily work? What about his home life? Answers to questions of this sort won't come easily or quickly or in a large public gathering. A person's deepest life needs can be discovered only on a one-to-one basis.

Paul dealt with the Thessalonians individually. He reminded them in his letter "how we were exhorting and encouraging and imploring *each one* of you as a father would his own children" (1 Thessalonians 2: 11). Going to large meetings is not enough. Listening to stirring sermons is not enough. Reading good books is not enough. Each member of the Body should have individual nurture and love if his real condition is to be perceived and his needs met. New believers, like babies, don't reach maturity on an assembly line.

What sort of believers are we trying to produce? Not

primarily gospel workers. Not primarily talkers-to-men.
Not primarily functionaries in the various Christian activities. No, our primary object is to produce mature men
and women whose ordinary stations and positions in life
can be transformed into platforms for ministry, for maintaining this earth according to God's plan, for shedding
God's light and love in an embittered world full of darkness and self love. But producing such believers will be
costly in time and labor. Where can we find the time and
the manpower for so much individual attention and care?

Jesus planted the answer to this question, in seed form,
within the Great Commission. He told His remaining
eleven disciples to "make disciples" (Matthew 28: 19).
What does disciple-making mean? Probably the shortest
and clearest statement on disciple-making is contained in
Paul's second letter to Timothy: "And the things which
you have heard from me in the presence of many witnesses, these entrust to faithful men, who will be able to
teach others also" (2 Timothy 2: 2). God's method is that
the church equip disciples who will equip disciples who
will equip disciples . . . . Why, then, are so few giving the
individual time and attention needed in teaching Christians how to live and work in the world? Can it be that
God's plan for church leadership isn't adequate to meet all
the needs? Or is it possible that our vision of God's plan
falls short?

Ask an ordinary Christian if he has ever considered
whether God might want to use him as a pastor, and you
may get a response like this: "Who, me? I've never at-
tended seminary or Bible school. All my experience has
been in secular work. So, you see, I could never be a
pastor." With allowances for local variations, this man's
response might well represent our corporate vision of
church leadership. But does God's idea of a pastor match
ours?

The term "pastors" used in Ephesians 4: 11 means "shepherds." Several Old Testament scriptures give us a fairly complete idea of the role of a pastor. For example, Ezekiel 34 makes it plain that a shepherd of God's people does about the same things on the spiritual plane that a shepherd of literal sheep would do: he feeds the flock; tends the sick ones; retrieves the strays; protects the flock from its enemies; and keeps the sheep from scattering. In short, the "pastors" or "shepherds" serve as those who watch over God's people and care for their needs.

Is this shepherding role limited to those we normally refer to as "pastors"? Peter supplies the answer: "I exhort the *elders* among you . . . shepherd the flock of God. . ." (1 Peter 5: 1, 2). According to Scripture, church elders are "pastors," because they are charged with shepherding duties, they are to watch over the people of God. This matter of watching over the Church brings to mind another title of church leadership used in the New Testament: that of "overseer" (or "bishop" as translated in the King James Version). This term comes from a root word meaning "to look at" or "to inspect," and recalls the "watchmen" of the Old Testament (Jeremiah 6: 17) or the church leaders in the New Testament who "keep watch over your souls" (Hebrews 13: 17). Most of a shepherd's job involves watching on behalf of the flock. By watching he observes the need for food, water, medicine,correction, or protection.

Did God intend that "pastors," and "elders," and "overseers" be separated into three classes of church leaders? For the answer we can listen to Paul as he speaks in Miletus. Paul had decided "to sail past Ephesus in order that he might not have to spend time in Asia; for he was hurrying to be in Jerusalem, if possible, on the day of Pentecost. And from Miletus he sent to Ephesus and called to him the *elders* of the church" (Acts 20: 16, 17).

What did he tell these elders? "Be on guard for yourselves and for all the flock, among which the Holy Spirit has made you *overseers* [bishops], to *shepherd* [pastor] the church of God which He purchased with His own blood" (v. 28). Paul told these elders that the Holy Spirit had made them overseers, and that their responsibility was to shepherd God's people. Clearly, "pastors," "elders," and "overseers," are not three separate categories of leadership, but simply three terms used to describe various facets of the same job.

Throughout the New Testament the consistent pattern is that each church had several such shepherds. Paul and Barnabas "appointed elders [plural] . . . in every church" (Acts 14: 23). When he wrote to Titus, Paul instructed him to "appoint elders [plural] in every city . . ." (Titus 1: 5). James wrote that a believer who was sick should "call for the elders [plural] of the church, and let them pray over him" (James 5:14). No distinction in rank is made between these elders, because Scripture recognizes only one Chief Shepherd, Jesus Christ Himself (1 Peter 5: 4).

What about the qualifications of these leaders? Paul gave Timothy some very explicit guidance in this matter. "An overseer, then, must be above reproach, the husband of one wife, temperate, prudent, respectable, hospitable, able to teach, not addicted to wine or pugnacious, but gentle, uncontentious, free from the love of money. He must be one who manages his own household well, keeping his children under control with all dignity (but if a man does not know how to manage his own household, how will he take care of the church of God?); and not a new convert, lest he become conceited and fall into the condemnation incurred by the devil. And he must have a good reputation with those outside the church, so that he may not fall into reproach and the snare of the devil." (1 Timothy 3: 2–7). The scriptural qualifications given for elders in Titus 1: 5–9 are virtually identical.

Where, in the scriptural standards, do we find any ground for our modern-day criteria for pastors? Does God require seminary or Bible school training for His shepherds? No. Does God direct that His shepherds bear the title, "Reverend"? No. Does He specify that all such shepherds must leave ordinary employment? No. Instead, we find that church leaders, first of all, must be men whose lives have been shaped by the Word of God. The scriptural criteria are very practical and down-to-earth. The way a man treats his own body, his wife, his children, other believers, and non-believers serves as the "fruit test" to be used in determining whether one is qualified to be a church leader or not.

There is one additional requirment: he must be able to teach God's truth. A man's life may be godly in every way, yet if God has not granted him the ability to teach, he would be limited as an overseer. (This helps to explain the close linking of "pastors and teachers" in Ephesians 4: 11). We find, then, that God's specifications for church leaders are on quite a different basis than ours. We look for outward appearances: education, titles. God looks to the heart. He looks for men in whom His Word has become flesh in practical, day-to-day living.

The man-made qualifications are restrictive, tending to cut down on the number of shepherds. Not many are able to attend Bible schools or seminaries once their careers have been launched. Not many can leave their ordinary employments. Many have no desire to erect a barrier between themselves and their brothers in Christ by assuming a title which suggests that they are to be reverenced above other men. On the other hand, God's qualifications are within the reach of many earnest Christians. Paul told Timothy that "if *any* man aspires to the office of overseer, it is a fine work he desires to do" (1 Timothy

3: 1). Any man! When it comes to church leadership, human qualifications keep men out. God's qualifications invite men in.

If we are serious about carrying out Jesus' command to make disciples, we will equip men to take real shepherding roles in the church without requiring them to become professional clergymen. Scripturally patterned disciple-making is God's plan for providing the time and individual attention needed to bring His children to maturity. One or two shepherds per flock cannot handle the load. Either we follow the heavenly pattern, or the work will not get done.

If our first need is to equip a number of pastors, how do we recognize the men of God's choosing? We have seen that Paul instructed Timothy that "if any man *aspires* to the office of overseer, it is a fine work he *desires* to do." One of the first questions, then, is: "Does such and such a brother want pastoral responsibility?" If God has not awakened in him a desire for such work, he should not be pressured to undertake it. But assuming that a number of men have the desire to become shepherds of God's people, how are we to discern whether it is God or their own self-interest calling them to it? We have previously referred to scriptures which list qualifications for overseers and elders (1 Timothy 3: 2–7; Titus 1: 5–9). These and a prayerful dependence upon the Holy Spirit's direction should guide our decisions in selecting church leaders.

A pastor who works full time at an ordinary job may possibly find his widest avenue of service there. His role as shepherd should not be confined to the group he meets with on Sundays. If there are members of the Body of Christ in his shop or office, what is to prevent such a man from serving them as a shepherd? If we are willing to die to the self-life of our group, we should be willing to share our shepherding service with the whole Body of Christ in our community. The ministry of such a man, of course, will not resemble our usual idea of the pastor's role. He would probably not conduct weddings or funerals. Nor would he coordinate a Christian group's programs. He might share a message now and then in his group's assembly, but probably would find his main service on a one-to-one and small group level. As one fully engaged in an ordinary vocation, this pastor could serve as a living model to believers working near him—carrying out the command to elders to be "examples to the flock" (1 Peter 5: 3).

Would such an arrangement leave a place for the pastors who devote full time to shepherding work? Of course. For example, such men would be in excellent positions to continue the work Paul assigned to Timothy, that of discipling others who could in turn disciple others. With an ever-expanding corps of shepherds, a group would soon be able to give the individual care and attention so essential in bringing believers to maturity.

But even here we must not step ahead of the Church's Head. Not all men are called or gifted to be shepherds. One who is not meant for this ministry should not be made to feel that his is a second-rate role in the Body of Christ. No, our ultimate goal is not even the production of more pastors, elders, or teachers, necessary as these are. Rather, the goal is mature believers—Christians in whom the life of Christ has formed in substantial measure. We should not expect dramatic, flashy, outwardly impressive believers to result from all this. People in whom Christ has formed will simply be servants. This one will occupy one position in the work world, that one will occupy another. But each will have learned how to convert his position in life into a place of service to God, to other Christians, and to mankind in general.

What would a mature believer in ordinary work be like? Will there be any indicators to assure us that we are reaching our goal? Remembering that our God is the master of infinite variety, we know that no two mature Christians will be identical. Some will produce thirtyfold, some sixtyfold, and some a hundredfold (Matthew 13: 8). We should also keep in mind that "there are varieties of gifts, but the same Spirit. And there are varieties of ministries, and the same Lord. And there are varieties of effects, but the same God who works all things in all persons" (1 Corinthians 12: 4–6). Even so, there ought to be some fairly recognizable common denominators by which we may "measure" how well we are achieving our aim. What will characterize the mature believer who works in the world?

Such a man will worship God in spirit and in truth, not just occasionally in public, but continuously in private. A man of prayer. A man who knows the Scriptures and delights in meditating upon them. He will pattern his work after what he sees of God's work.

He will see that ordinary work is just as essential as gospel work. He will have a large and lasting vision of God's purposes in positioning him in his job.

Such a man will not consider himself to be "just a layman." Rather, he will know himself to be one of that company through whom "the manifold wisdom of God might now be made known . . . to the rulers and the authorities in the heavenly places" (Ephesians 3: 10).

He will recognize the evils in Babylon, but will not shun the world for that reason. The world will not overcome him, but he will overcome the world. The life of Christ within him will touch the unclean and make it clean.

Because of his good works on the job others will be forced to praise God, in this life and when judgment comes.

This man will welcome the hardships, struggles, and disappointments which come via his job as sent by God to form Christ within him. He will thank God for his tests and trials at work. He will realize that God's work *in* him must always precede God's work *through* him.

As he is broken, and as God's light breaks through him, this man will serve the other members of Christ's Body who are near him at work. He will love them, forgive them, pray for them, share with them—even give his life for them if called upon by God to do that—without regard to which congregations these brothers and sisters may meet with on Sundays.

He will be a man who sees the Church, not in terms of his group, but in terms of the Body of Christ in his community and in the world. He will make it his habit to assemble with other Christians, both to help build them up and to be built up by them.

This man will long to see unbelieving co-workers turn from sin to follow Christ. He will pray for them, live Christ before them, and always be ready to speak the good news of salvation through faith in Christ with freshness and in love.

He will be a man whose heart-soul-mind-strength love for God will be translated into the language of everyday action—loving action toward his fellow-men. He will respect earthly authority, yielding obedience to his employer, honoring him.

As this man does his daily work wholeheartedly, "as to the Lord," he consciously will be carrying out God's first command, to subdue and rule over the earth and its creatures. He will know that this is a holy calling.

He will be a man whose work is not his god, who knows how and when to lay down his tools to care for the needs of his family and others.

This man will know equally well how to work and how to rest. For he will have received the gift of soul-rest from above, the peace that surpasses understanding.

He will not be ruled by his wages. Instead, even his

money will be converted into "kingdom currency," and put to uses approved by God. He will not expect full pay for his efforts in this life, but will know how to lay up an investment in heaven.

The spiritual man in ordinary work will look forward to the day of his liberation, when Jesus Christ will appear to those who are looking for His return. This man will rest in the fact that Christ has promised to call those sons of God working in the field, grinding at the mill, or laboring in whatever occupation to which He may have assigned them. On that day, this man knows, he will receive the reward for his service, "knowing that whatever good thing each one does, this he will receive back from the Lord, whether slave or free" (Ephesians 6: 8).

Patiently, this man will be willing to wait for his real reward, the sheer joy of hearing his heavenly Employer welcome him home with the words: "Well done, good and faithful slave; you were faithful with a few things, I will put you in charge of many things, enter into the joy of your master" (Matthew 25: 21).